"Rachel Srubas deftly juxtaposes pithy w[...]
Fathers with intensely personal reflections on both ordinary and colorful people and events in her own life. Her painfully honest, practical and lyrical, poignant and occasionally funny anecdotes, touch the heart while delighting the mind of anyone who appreciates skillfully chosen words. Each of the forty essays is a model and a tacit appeal for the reader's own personal reflection."

Sr. Lenora Black, OSB
Editor of *Spirit & Life* magazine

"I admire the warmth and candor with which Rachel writes about spiritual life in the everyday world. The book would make a fine, reassuring companion on a Lenten journey or on any other 40-day sojourn in the 'desert' of Christian contemplation of the Holy."

Nancy Mairs
Writer
Tucson, Arizona

"The title of Barbara Brown Taylor's recent book, *Leaving Church*, has become an icon of sorts for people who are finding the difficulties and discouragements of church life a burden. Rachel Srubas offers a refreshingly new (yet old) response to such difficulties and discouragements. Drawing on St. Benedict and his mentors, the desert fathers and mothers, Srubas offers a model for how to pay attention to our own responses, using Scripture, prayer, and ancient wisdom to learn practical virtues in the daily living of our lives, especially in the uncomfortable moments. Like Benedict himself, Srubas has learned to be at home with human weakness, even as she delights in 'the Gospel's outlandish promises and demands, and its huge hope.' *City of Prayer* is a wonderful and down-to-earth mystic's recipe for spiritual growth!"

Norvene Vest
Spiritual Director and Author

City of Prayer

Forty Days with Desert Christians

Rachel M. Srubas

LITURGICAL PRESS
Collegeville, Minnesota

www.litpress.org

Cover design by David Manahan, OSB. Photo provided by dreamstime.com, © Kawalec.

1	2	3	4	5	6	7	8

Library of Congress Cataloging-in-Publication Data

Srubas, Rachel M.
    City of prayer : forty days with desert Christians / Rachel M. Srubas.
        p.   cm.
    Includes bibliographical references.
    ISBN 978-0-8146-3095-2 (pbk.)
    1. Meditations.   2. Desert Fathers.   3. Monastic and religious life of women.   4. Women in Christianity.   I. Title.

BV4832.3.S685 2008
242—dc22

2008008179

With love for my mother and father,
Alice Tarpinian Srubas and John Richard Srubas

and for Jean Carol Bronson,
who is a Desert Mother to many.

Contents

Acknowledgments

I give thanks to Ken S. McAllister, who cheers me up and cheers me on and loves me always; to my dear family; to Alex Hendrickson and her family; to Lenora Black, OSB, and all Benedictine Sisters of Perpetual Adoration, in whose magazine, *Spirit and Life* an earlier version of the poem "City of Prayer" and the essay "Iona Stone" first appeared; to Lonni Pearce; to Marney Wasserman; to Jonel and Frank Martinez and family; to Sherry Gregg; to Antigone Bookstore; to all the congregations I have loved and served, and especially to the people of Mountain Shadows Presbyterian Church; to the staff of the Collegeville Institute for Ecumenical and Cultural Research, the monks of Saint John's Abbey, and the participants in "Writing and the Pastoral Life"; to the Lilly Endowment, Inc.; to Hans Christoffersen and the staff of Liturgical Press; to John Mogabgab, editor of *Weavings: A Journal of the Christian Spiritual Life*, in which a version of the essay "Good Vigilantes" first appeared; to Teresa Blythe and the staff and participants in the Hesychia School of Spiritual Direction; to Fran Buss; to Patricia Casey; to Rose Taul; to Annick Safken; to Maha Baddar; to Joanne Moses; to Judd Ruggill and Justine Hernandez; to Sharon Nicks and the World Community for Christian Meditation in Tucson, Arizona; to my colleagues in Presbytery de Cristo; to the Oblates of St. Benedict of Tucson, Arizona and elsewhere; to Sister Diane Bridenbecker, OP; to Melanie Supan Groseta; to Ken again, with love.

Actual persons powerfully shaped my writing of this work. In some cases, in order to protect individuals' privacy, I have altered names and details or have composed composite characters representing my perception and experience of multiple persons. Pastoral ethics mandate that, prior to publication, a pastor who is also an author obtain the permission of any parishioners whose stories are to appear in a book. I have gratefully obtained such permissions from parishioners, and from other family members, friends, and associates, all of whom have blessed me and my writing with their generous, unhesitating encouragement.

Rachel M. Srubas

Introduction

Christianity Is a Desert Religion

Discovering the Desert

Two summers into our marriage, my husband Ken and I drove from Chicago to Colorado, to camp in the Rocky Mountains. Initially we pitched our tent at such a high elevation that we panted for lack of oxygen and woke up to snow. So we drove some distance down the mountain and found, at the end of a dirt road, a campsite called The Commissary. A cold, stony creek splashed past it and sunlight made its way through the pines—when rain wasn't falling, which it did with regularity. This made dry firewood hard to find. Our days in the Rockies were made just that—rocky—by the clean, high, and changeable weather. One morning, in the rainwater that had collected in one of our cooking pots, we discovered that a mouse had drowned. That did it. Now we weren't merely out of our urban element, we were dangerous to other living beings.

Before the rains could return and muck up Commissary Road, making it impassable, we shoved our gear into our aging Toyota and rolled out of there. Some miles outside of Gunnison we came upon a house with a hand-lettered sign in front advertising two-dollar hot showers, cold drinks, and candy bars. I felt a little nervous about the taciturn cowboy minding the store, but Ken kept his eye on him. The shower stall was cramped and the water pressure minimal, but it was enough to get me clean.

It's been said that America does its best thinking in the shower. I washed my hair and thought about Interstate 25. The highway atlas showed it running right out of Colorado, southward to New Mexico. Neither Ken nor I had ever been there, but I liked the "New" part of its name. It sounded promising. And "Mexico"—that sounded sunny and dry.

Hours later, soon after we had crossed state lines, the warm, arid wind rushing in through the car windows pulled the waves out of my hair. The terrain went scrubby and the sky enormous, with rows of dollop-clouds receding into the distance, reminding me of a painting I'd seen at the Art Institute of Chicago. By the next afternoon we had turned onto a highway that wound among yellow mesas bigger than the buildings that flanked Michigan Avenue back home. We stopped for a picnic of canned deviled ham spread on "desert toast," which is what our bread became after seconds of exposure to the warm, waterless breezes.

We set up camp in northern New Mexico and learned some essentials. For instance, the waitress at the Spic & Span Diner was talking about chile—marvelous piquant sauce made from peppers—when she asked you, "red or green?" And the rains still rolled in around four o'clock every afternoon, but plunging through the desert air changed them qualitatively. By the time the drops hit the earth you appreciated the way they pummeled the sagebrush until its scent broke open. Living things needed water, which was scarce and holy here and not to be complained about. We would sit in our car, buffered by the air and rubber of its tires, and watch lightning pulse and crack on the horizon. We thought about the desert's snakes and lizards waiting out the storm in their underground dwellings.

Pretty soon the rain would stop, the sandy soil and the parched air had sucked away all water, and in the twilight a few bats would appear overhead, darting after insects. The sky would darken, dissolving the mountains' silhouettes, and stars would emerge in far greater numbers than we city dwellers had realized existed. A few stars even shot across heaven. Awestruck, we lay on our backs on the Toyota's warm hood, watching the dynamic night while bugs the bats hadn't managed to catch buzzed and feasted on our ankles.

For the next several summers Ken and I made pilgrimage to the high desert of Northern New Mexico, which we had come to consider our salvation from Chicago's muggy, traffic-jammed corridors and the pressures of graduate school. As we grew to know the region, we learned we weren't the only ones for whom its ground was holy. First, of course, had been the Anasazi people who, centuries earlier, had made their homes among the cliffs. Pueblo people followed, and Mexican Americans, mainly Roman Catholic, some of whose descendants' immaculate low-rider cars bore airbrushed images of Nuestra Señora de Guadalupe on their hoods. Whole communities of Sikhs, Benedictines, Muslims, and Presbyterians had also settled in the high desert of Northern New Mexico, apparently having concluded, as we had done, that walking on the sandy soil, being dwarfed by great, rusty canyons, and breathing piñon-tinged air were conducive to prayer.

Gratefully, we would pitch our tent in the campground at Ghost Ranch, a Presbyterian conference center. Toward evening, when other campers were firing up their Coleman stoves, Ken and I would visit the men's and women's cinderblock shower rooms, respectively, checking the cool corners for wayward snakes and leaving undisturbed the long-legged spiders who wove their webs in the window frames. We loved the landscape and the earthy hospitality of Ghost Ranch, but sometimes we craved silence that we couldn't find in the center's purposeful workshops and busy dining hall.

Silence is a Benedictine specialty, and at the Benedictine Monastery of Christ in the Desert, situated miles down an unimproved road near the Chama River, the silence is rich and layered—anxiety-provoking to the unaccustomed. Nowadays the monastery boasts an elegant and spacious visitors' center, but when Ken and I visited there in the 1990s we bumped into each other in the monks' tiny gift and book shop. There I first discovered that monastic spirituality and desert spirituality were forms of Christian life that people had written about extensively, and even I, an urban Presbyterian, could practice these spiritualities in my way.

Benedict and His Desert Predecessors

The monks of Christ in the Desert live by the Rule of Saint Benedict, a slender, practical guide for contemplative life in community, written in the sixth century. A decade after I initially encountered Benedictine spirituality in Northern New Mexico, I published *Oblation*, a collection of prayers I had written, inspired by the gospel-infused wisdom of Benedict's Rule and by the prayerful, productive Benedictine Sisters of Tucson, Arizona, the Sonoran Desert city where Ken and I had come to make our home.

In the final chapter of the Rule—its epilogue—Benedict comments, "The purpose for which we have written this rule is to make it clear that by observing it in our monasteries we can at least achieve the first steps in virtue and good monastic practice. Anyone, however, who wishes to press on toward the highest standards of monastic life may turn to the teachings of the holy Fathers, which can lead those who follow them to the very heights of perfection."[1]

The "holy Fathers" to whom Benedict refers include, among others, Evagrius Ponticus, who was one of the first writers to record the sayings of desert-dwelling monastics of ancient Christendom, and John Cassian, whose *Institutes* and *Conferences* systematically present the organizing principles of third- and fourth-century desert monasteries and the spiritualities their residents practiced.

Loosely speaking, *City of Prayer* is the sequel to *Oblation*. The latter book consists of modern-day meditations on Benedict's sixth-century teachings. This collection of reflections applies to contemporary circumstances some insights of Benedict's desert predecessors—men and women who gained renown for their pithy teachings on prayer, solitude, silence, humility, and other essentials of contemplative Christian life. As an oblate—a non-monastic affiliate of the Order of St. Benedict (and a thoroughly fallible one, at that)—I may not have achieved even "the first steps in virtue and good monastic practice" of which Benedict speaks. Nevertheless, I wish, as he says, "to press on," if not to "the highest standards of monastic life," then to the next phase in my exploration of an ancient-yet-modern Christian spirituality that balances prayer and work, solitude and community, self-awareness and service, and above all, reverences God.

Different Deserts, One Faith

I live in the arid zone called Southern Arizona. This severe-yet-fragile Sonoran region—renowned for its Giant Saguaro cactuses, which stand as tall as mature trees and develop "arms" only after seventy-five years of growth—is a different desert from the one that originally beckoned to Ken and me by way of Interstate 25. The Sonoran Desert is also miles and millennia from the Sinai Desert to which thousands of contemplative Christians fled in the third and fourth centuries, essentially to invent Christian monasticism. But both the American Southwest and the North African plateaus are, to borrow Belden Lane's term, "fierce landscapes." My travels and my years of permanent residence in Tucson have taught me what desert dwellers know: high heat and hard earth, severe terrain overarched by burning sky, will drive you into rigorous communion with your Creator. The desert will show you what you are and are not made of, what you do and do not need.

The Sonoran borderlands in which I live claim a terrible fame. Every year thousands of economic migrants—impoverished, undocumented people in search of work and living wages—walk from Mexico into the United States through largely uninhabited areas, and in appalling numbers die of exposure and dehydration. Some Christians of Tucson express their faith through efforts to change immigration legislation, or by placing tanks of drinking water in some of the hottest, most highly trafficked and deadly stretches of desert. While I honor these ministries, I cannot claim them as my own.

I pastor a Presbyterian church north of Tucson, at the base of the Santa Catalina Mountains, in a rapidly developing residential and commercial area. As I drive to church and look out at housing and business developments clustered amid cacti and creosote bushes in the shadows of a rugged mountain range, I recall famous words of Athansius, a fourth-century writer. He said of his monastic contemporaries, thousands of whom had ventured beyond the Nile Valley to inhabit a landscape more barren than Southern Arizona's, that they had "made the desert a city."

It would be unrealistic to suggest too close a comparison between ancient Desert Fathers and Mothers and today's general population of Southern Arizona. The lifestyle of residents living in the "master planned communities" and humbler manufactured homes near my church differs dramatically from that of ancient desert monastics. The Desert Fathers and Mothers could not have dreamed of such a present-day desert "necessity" as centralized cooling, but had this luxury been available to them they would have shunned it as an indulgent obstacle to the austere existence they pursued in order to draw closer to God.

Still, meaningful connections may be made between modern and ancient desert people of faith. For example, about ninety minutes' drive from Tucson, at the end of an unmarked road, a Greek Orthodox monastery, established in 1995, is dedicated to St. Anthony the Great. There a community of men obedient to an abbot hold all their possessions in common and devote their lives to a rigorous schedule of liturgical and private prayer and manual work. The monastery's namesake, Abba Anthony, a Desert Father who lived in Alexandria, Egypt in the third and fourth centuries, is sometimes described as the founder of Western monasticism. Anthony's biographer is the same

Athanasius who remarked on the monastic, urban transformation of Egypt's previously uninhabited regions.

"We must not forget that Christianity is a desert religion and therefore shaped by this environment. . . . The desert is honed down to essentials and requires the same of those living there." So writes the Oblate Master of Pluscarden Abbey in Elgin, Morayshire, Scotland, in a letter to Benedictine Oblates concerning "ceaseless prayer." In Mark Salzman's elegant, insightful novel of monastic life called *Lying Awake*, a Carmelite Sister observes that "the desert is what you bring to it, a landscape of the heart."

The Scottish Benedictine and the fictional Carmelite make roughly the same point: whether or not you practice your Christian faith amid the austerities of a physical desert, if you sincerely follow Jesus you will come to relinquish cushioning superfluities and learn the truth of who you are and who is the God on whom you utterly depend. "The Christian life is the same for everyone," notes Georgios I. Mantzarides, author of an article on orthodox monasticism to which the web site for St. Anthony's Greek Orthodox Monastery of Florence, Arizona is linked.

Because the Christian life, this desert religion, *is* ultimately the same for everyone—Orthodox, Roman Catholic, and Protestant, ancient and modern alike—and because Christians bring what we will to our navigations of the heart's landscape and lose what we must along the way, the sayings of those early Christian teachers, the Desert Fathers and Mothers, remain compelling many centuries after they were originally uttered and heard.

Forty Desert Days

The late twentieth and early twenty-first centuries saw the publication of numerous anthologies of sayings attributed to the Desert Fathers and Mothers. Also readily available to readers is a variety of commentaries, introductory as well as academic, on these ancient Christian teachings. In *City of Prayer* I don't presume to add to the scholarly corpus, but offer instead one modern Christian voice, reflecting personally, honestly, and—I hope—faithfully on the implications of some forty sayings of the Desert Fathers and Mothers; a great many more such sayings exist. I hope to add to the expanding bibliography on desert spirituality the voice of one practitioner whose personal reflections on everyday matters of Christian faith and ministry, prompted by forty sayings of our ancient forebears, may encourage present-day readers to ground their spiritual lives in the wisdom of Christianity's most enduring teachers.

I am a preacher, and while they aren't sermons, the reflections in these pages make a homiletic move or two; they apply early Christian wisdom to modern life and encourage faithfulness to God as revealed by Jesus, whose forty-day wilderness sojourn sets the example for all Christians who would practice a spirituality shaped by the demands of the desert. *City of Prayer* may make for fitting reading during the weeks that lead to Easter. But just as the Desert Fathers and Mothers practiced their prayerful faith in all seasons, so might readers of this collection take it up at any time in the Christian year. Likewise, the reflections, each of which is self-contained, may be read in any order. Their relative brevity makes them suitable for inclusion in morning or evening devotions, while the reflections' candor may encourage spiritual book discussion group members to share their own lives' stories and interpretations of early Christians' sayings.

Jesus was confronted in the desert by the demons of idolatry, self-indulgence, and self-aggrandizement. Like many followers of Jesus, I, too, struggle with these and other temptations, as will become apparent in the reflections to follow. One Desert Mother, Amma Syncletica, said, "we . . . must kindle the divine fire in ourselves through tears and hard work."[2] In *City of Prayer* I recount some of my tears and hard work, and reflect as a pastor and spiritual practitioner on various dimensions of the life of faith in order to serve as an authentic, if imperfect, companion to readers seeking to go where Jesus leads and learn from some of his earliest, most trustworthy followers.

The Desert Fathers and Mothers renounced and retreated from the decadence of Roman culture to emulate, for the rest of their lives, Jesus' forty post-baptismal days in the Judean desert. The Abbas and Ammas (as the Fathers and Mothers were called) aspired to ceaseless, soul-changing prayer made possible by God's grace and their own freedom from excessive activity, socializing, noise, distraction, possessions, and pride. While some Desert Christians practiced extreme physical austerity and cultivated shame as though it were a virtue, the wisest ones pursued moderation in all things and balanced their solitary prayer with purposeful labor and availability to the spiritual pilgrims who visited them, seeking guidance, asking, "Give me a word." They have much to teach present-day people who hunger for a prayerful, transformational relationship with God that integrates solitude, silence, attentiveness, healthy humility, simplicity, and service.

I consider myself a present-day pilgrim and protégé of the Desert Mothers and Fathers. The road I have traveled to find them is paved with books. I give thanks especially for the numerous works of Benedicta Ward, SLG, a respected compiler and translator of early Christian monastics' sayings whose books, *The Sayings of the Desert Fathers* and *The Desert Fathers* I gratefully quote frequently and commend to readers; for Laura Swan, OSB, author of *The Forgotten Desert Mothers: Sayings, Lives, and Stories of Early Christian Women*, from which I also gratefully quote passages; for Mary Forman, OSB, whose *Praying with the Desert Mothers* is both learned and practical; and for David G. R. Keller, whose *Oasis of Wisdom* lucidly contextualizes the Desert Fathers and Mothers in history, place, culture, and spiritual tradition.

The Desert Fathers and Mothers preceded by roughly two centuries even Saint Benedict, who lived over fifteen hundred years ago. Yet Benedict's rule of life continues to exert a remarkable influence on an ecumenical and international array of Christians. Comparably, Benedict's instructive desert predecessors speak, sometimes prophetically, to a present generation of spiritual practitioners searching for ways to keep the faith

and keep it simple amid a culture of individualism, domination, greed, consumption, and exploitation. The sayings of the
Desert Fathers and Mothers offer incisive antidotes to a hum-
ming, numbing climate of excess in which the overscheduling of
time crowds out contemplation and the overvaluing of personal
achievement underestimates the sovereignty of God.

When Jesus, ravenous and parched at the end of his forty
Spirit-led desert days, was tempted to trade in his faithfulness for unlimited personal power, God and his faith in God
strengthened him to withstand devilish enticements. Surely
God also led Jesus' earliest monastic followers into the desert
and sustained and taught them there. Two thousand years later
and counting, present-day disciples of Jesus will be inspired,
challenged, and comforted by the Desert Fathers' and Mothers'
perseverance, counsel, and prayer.

In the fourth century, Christianity gained acceptance
and became the official religion of the Roman Empire.
As Christianity moved into the mainstream, the movement toward the desert and monastic life increased. The
desert was a place for quieting the inner noise that kept
[people] from hearing the whispers of God.

Laura Swan, OSB, *The Forgotten Desert Mothers*

Once a brother went to visit his sister who was ill in a
nunnery. She was someone of great faith. She commanded
him, "Go away, my brother, and pray for me, for by Christ's
grace I shall see you in the kingdom of heaven."

The Desert Fathers:
Sayings of the Early Christian Monks

City of Prayer

Soon after the baptismal waters had dried
on the Emperor Constantine's skin,
underground Christians emerged
from their homes and catacombs,
blinking, barely believing
the revolution in Rome. High above
the sewage in the streets
and pantheistic palace-temples,
a basilica arose, domed and gleaming,
designed by imperial architects to impress Christ.
He, invisible, risen, kept busy
blessing the slaves who broke their backs
building this glorious church.

When the workers could no longer lift
the emperor's travertine slabs,
they returned to the shadows
where once they had hidden
in worshipful remembrance of Jesus,
the stonemason's son, God's beloved.
He, who had overcome his own crucifixion,
would surely come to save them.

But the bright sunlight of born-again Rome
had made Christ unrecognizable
to the catacomb Christians.
They set out by night for Egypt, Arabia, Syria, Palestine,
deserts for which prophets and penitents
had always been destined. These ragged Romans
were in for the Lent of their lives.
All the temptations they tried
to leave behind followed them
into their new, cryptic solitudes,
where, among scorpions, demons, and dunes,
they fought their way to salvation.

Whole pilgrim-populations followed,
and the stony wilderness was turned

into a city of prayer.
Centuries later, I seek my own path there,
to hear for myself, to try to understand
the blistering command and assurance
of one Desert Mother whose name
no one remembers:

> *Go away,* she whispers, *and pray for me.*
> *I shall see you in the kingdom of heaven.*

– Day 1 –
I Could Say as Much to You

Amma Theodora said, "A devout person happened to be insulted by someone, and replied, 'I could say as much to you but the commandment of God keeps my mouth shut.'"

The Forgotten Desert Mothers, 66

In the Sonoran Desert, February is a sweet month. Pale, late winter sunlight floods the Santa Catalina Mountains, which rise up, grand and craggy, east of the church I pastor. From the window in my office I can see the lower elevations of these mountains. They're reassuring, like an elder who has seen it all and watches out for you, protective but sufficiently humble and wise to keep quiet as you make your own way in the world.

It was the afternoon of Ash Wednesday, and I hadn't yet composed the words I would say to the handful of parishioners who would gather for worship that evening. The day was so bright and beautiful I found it hard to feel penitentially Lenten, or even introspective. Back in Chicago, Ash Wednesday would have been a cold, slogging affair, a short gray day on which even a brief examination of conscience would readily reveal the soul's gutters to be clogged with the wet and blackened leaves of impasse and regret, packed under grimy, weeks-old snow. I sat staring at Psalm 51, waiting for guidance, but its

1

language of sinfulness and purification seemed irrelevant to the mild day at hand.

My mobile phone rang. Although I felt I shouldn't take a call just now, with the Ash Wednesday homily as yet unwritten, I answered. It's a bittersweet privilege to be the friend a friend can call to blurt, "I am so mortified, I feel like crawling into a hole."

My caller, my dear friend, was at that time navigating a delicate, uncertain period in her vocation and career. In a voice flattened by shock, but with her characteristic honesty and a helping of profanity, she told me the story, which, later on, she recounted discreetly on her blog, changing names, disguising details.

My friend's story went like this: a respected, elder colleague, Linda, had telephoned her. "She proceeds to tell me that a mutual colleague, Seth, had a 'concern' about me. Seth is a bit of a peacock and know-it-all. Evidently, he came to Linda about a specific . . . criticism of me . . . along the lines of, 'Seth thinks you should quit sweating so much.' A cut-me-to-the-bone kind of rejection of a fairly essential part of who I am. Something that I can't really imagine changing. Something necessary and vital to my life and vocation. My mouth hung open as Linda talked. I quickly thanked her for her concerns and got off the phone."

As I held my own phone to my ear, my friend's embarrassment and pain cast a shadow across the sunlit day, the way Ash Wednesday casts a shadow across a still-new year, or ashes, ritually applied, disfigure a clean forehead. *Remember that you are dust* is the message my friend had received, unexpectedly, harshly, unfairly. Who could blame her if she had returned the insult, retorting, "And to dust, Linda, *you* shall return"? But she did not return evil for evil, as if restrained by the commandment of God to which Amma Theodora refers: "A devout person happened to be insulted by someone, and replied, 'I could say as much to you but the commandment of God keeps my mouth shut.'"

On Ash Wednesday and on every other day of our lives we are all of us dust—inconsequential by most standards, and eventually, by death, sure to be wiped clean off the face of the earth. This does not mean we need hurtful reminders of our fragility. Even people who behave in pompous and cowardly ways, as did the pseudonymous Seth, exploiting a third party to deliver a mean blow, warrant basic respect. As all of us have, Seth has surely taken some devastating hits in his own life. What else would explain his connivance and passive aggression? Wounded, unhealed souls are often those who find it impossible to practice what Theodora preaches, and keep their big mouths shut.

My friend concluded her blog posting with these words: "I don't know why Linda decided to participate in this triangulated situation with Seth. I am going to do everything in my power to ignore it. Because my power is pretty weak, I would covet your prayers. My Lenten journey for this year involves letting go and not forcing other people to act the way that I think is right and proper. This is not to say that my feelings are not extremely bruised and tender."

A few hours after concluding my afternoon phone conversation with my friend, I smeared ashes on the tender foreheads of the worshipers who had assembled at my church. But first, I read them a poem I had written.

To Number Our Days

. . . In all that we do we try to present ourselves as ministers of God, acting with patient endurance amid trials, difficulties, distresses, beatings, imprisonments and riots; in hard work, sleepless nights, and hunger.

2 Corinthians 6:4-5

Tonight, the liturgy of grit—
the ashen smudge of finitude
thumbed onto your forehead.
Tonight, you join the communion
of disciples who hurried off to church

just to be reminded of their brevity on earth,
and accept the creaturely, Christian bruise
of a dirty cross above the eyes.
Why? Why put ourselves through
this grim ritual and terrifying talk
of dust and dying?

In all that we do we try
to present ourselves as ministers of God,
acting with patient endurance amid trials.

You and the faithful remnant
go forward for your annual defacement.
As you make your way back to the pews,
you're aware that carbon particles—
the stuff that dust
and all of us are made of—
are settling on your eyebrows,
darkening your outlook.

You look around
at the small congregation of faces,
all bearing the same shadowy mark:
our Creator's single, stark initial,
spelling out the story of our lives.

– Day 2 –
Work and Pray

When the holy Abba Anthony lived in the desert, he was beset by *accidie*, and attacked by many sinful thoughts. He said to God, "Lord, I want to be saved but these thoughts do not leave me alone; what shall I do in my affliction? How can I be saved?" A short while afterwards, when he got up to go out, Anthony saw a man like himself, sitting at his work, getting up from his work to pray, then sitting down and plaiting a rope, then getting up again to pray. It was an angel of the Lord sent to correct and reassure him. He heard the angel saying to him, "Do this and you will be saved." At these words, Anthony was filled with joy and courage. He did this, and he was saved.

The Sayings of the Desert Fathers, 1–2

Students of monastic spirituality and early Christian history revere Abba Anthony as a holy man—a saint, in fact. Having lived in the desert of third-century Egypt, Anthony is known as "The Father of Monks," the originator of monasticism in the Western world. It may surprise you, then, to learn that Anthony struggled with *accidie*, which is traditionally translated as "sloth." What this means is that at times Anthony found it so hard to get himself going, to focus his mind and accomplish his goals, that he was driven to ask for God's help. He may

5

even have lost sight of his life's purpose, and wondered what he was living for. Not only that, but "many sinful thoughts" attacked him. He felt so besieged by preoccupations that he was unable to pursue his deepest desire: to know the love and mercy of God.

Sound familiar? Maybe so. Many of us turn to books like the one in your hands when we are struggling with the very difficulties Anthony faced. We long for God. We want to live a life in which we enjoy an awareness of the sacred, loving relationships, personal well-being, and meaningful work in the service of a shared hope for the world. But at times we find it hard to get off the couch. We intend to develop our inner lives, but we veg out instead, watching reruns on TV, avoiding the very thing we long for, and then berating ourselves for being lazy and unproductive, "not spiritual enough."

A friend of mine—a gifted woman of faith who can at times be very hard on herself—has a simple name for merciless self-criticism and other negative ruminations: "Bad Mind." It seems that even Saint Anthony of Egypt suffered from Bad Mind. It was not some innate perfection that eventually led Anthony to sainthood; it was his creative and faithful struggle against the same difficult internal forces—sapped enthusiasm and mental malignancy—that beset you and me at times. We can tell from Anthony's prayer that he yearned to be saved, and not only in the hereafter. In the here-and-now Anthony ached for salvation from the deep fatigue and maddening anxieties that kept him from communing wholeheartedly with God.

And then, one day, Anthony saw a man going about his life in a very different spirit from Anthony's own discouragement and desperation. The man worked, braiding fibers, perhaps derived from water reeds, into rope. He would get up periodically to pray, and then return to his efforts. Anthony saw the man as an angel not because a luminous aura surrounded him but because he showed Anthony a way through his dilemma. "Do this," the man said, "and you will be saved." Did he mean that Anthony, too, should become a rope maker? That would be too literal a reading of the scene. The man exemplified balance. He worked and prayed in equal measure. He didn't worry about himself, but rather performed a service, created a product that would be of use to others. And regularly he turned to face his Creator, to give thanks and seek guidance and blessing.

"Anthony was filled with joy and courage" because the solution to his problems was revealed as simple and clear. What would save Anthony from his physical lethargy and the quagmire of his thoughts would be to alternate his unworried engagement in practical tasks with acts of direct and sincere devotion to God. "He did this, and he was saved." As he worked, energy flowed back into his body. As he prayed, his mind became clear and unencumbered. He remembered who he was and whose he was. He cultivated a practice, a way of life that balanced work and prayer. Over time this freed him from torpor and self-defeat.

Today Anthony may be an angel sent by God to instruct and reassure you. The simple story of a great man who faithfully overcame the same spiritual difficulties you may face —discouragement and worry—is perhaps enough to restore your joy and encourage you. Your salvation is not something you must win by professing your formulaic assent to one religious tenet. Nor must you work to be saved. Your salvation is your daily experience of God's life-giving goodness. Anthony's story makes clear that by living a life in balance, by interspersing your active responsibilities with restorative reflection, you will avail yourself of God's saving grace.

– Day 3 –

A Desert Retreat

Matrona said, "Many solitaries living in the desert have been lost because they lived like people in the world. It is better to live in a crowd and want to live a solitary life than to live in solitude and be longing all the time for company."

The Desert Fathers, 11

What is on your calendar today, or tomorrow? Does the day stretch out before you, blessedly empty of obligations and deadlines, promising you solitude and peace? Or will you be running from appointment to appointment, scrambling to keep your commitments, going full speed until you drop, exhausted, at the end of the day? Or might your day consist of some happy medium between quiet contemplation and frenetic overactivity?

I write this reflection on a day in which I'm attempting to find that happy medium, although I'd prefer a day of total quiet. Let me tell you a little about this morning. It seems illustrative of the challenges many of us face in seeking time for peace and prayer in the midst of our busy lives.

Going on right now is a daylong meeting at which I've arranged to arrive late. I have made this arrangement in order to protect my writing time, which is an important spiritual practice for me. But as I sat down to write this morning, anxiety tugged at my mind and urged me to check my calendar. I discovered I had double-booked myself for one morning next week. At one and the same time I was scheduled to be present at a retreat center, teaching a class on *lectio divina* (the practice of monastic prayerful reading), *and* to be at the church I pastor on the other side of town, hosting a guest speaker, a gracious Muslim woman who has agreed to explain some basics of Islam to a group of interested Christians.

I have yet to learn how to clone myself or accomplish "bi-location." I cannot be in two places at once. In fact, I often try to avoid multitasking, because being present to the present moment is an important way to practice mindfulness in the midst of activity, to be attentive, aware, responsive to the movements of God's Spirit in the day's occurrences. But as I considered the conflict on my calendar the mindful quiet of this morning's writing time was quickly giving way to worry about how I would resolve my scheduling dilemma.

It was from Benedictines that I learned the approach to prayerful reading that I was scheduled to teach at the retreat center. I telephoned a Benedictine friend of mine, a longtime monastic Sister named Lenora, whose monastery is situated just two miles from my house. Lenora combines contemplative devotion to God with remarkable warmth and enthusiasm toward people. She agreed to substitute teach the class at the retreat center, explaining that she had no obligations at the monastery that day because it would be her designated "hermit day," a monthly day that members of her community usually reserve for solitary prayer.

Possibly, when Lenora fills in for me at the retreat center, teaching some twenty spiritual seekers the art of prayerful reading, a part of her will long for "the hermitage," the time alone she sacrificed in order to help a friend. "It is better," says Amma Matrona, "to live in a crowd and want to live a solitary life than to live in solitude and be longing all the time for company." According to this Desert Mother, by publicly engaging in the life of a learning community and perhaps hungering for a bit of reflective quiet, Sister Lenora will be doing what is preferable to maintaining a reluctant, lonely, and distracted solitude.

If you have ever made a silent retreat by yourself, perhaps you have relished the unstructured quiet, the freedom simply to be in God's presence. Or maybe, like many people unaccustomed to unscheduled hours empty of conversation, entertainment, and news, you have found the silence intimidating or boring. You haven't known what to do with yourself, or what the Spirit might be doing with you while you endure the slow and shapeless progression of hours. If you don't run away from solitude at the first signs of discomfort you can learn to be alone and keep quiet. You can learn to listen with your bones for secrets untold in noisy, busy places. You can learn to love the silence, which is the language God speaks, and learn to love yourself, the true and unpretentious self who emerges in the silence. You can even learn to long for solitude, to need places and periods when you and God simply dwell together, without cable television or mobile telephones.

As I write these words I imagine the serenity of a desert retreat house I have visited numerous times. I love to sit in the library there, with my back to books reassuringly shelved in orderly rows, facing windows that look out to rocky, golden soil, scrubby vegetation, and an unmarked sky. My yearning to get back there, Amma Matrona tells me, is a better thing than would be my dwelling there, itching to go to the mall or make a phone call.

Learn to long for a desert retreat of your own, whatever may be the particular geography where you live. You need not travel to Egypt or the American Southwest in order to experience the daunting, beckoning landscape of your interior desert, the place within you so quiet that you can hear cactus needles standing up to the wind and hear God dreaming your life. Believe Amma Matrona when she tells you it's a good thing to yearn for such silence, such solitude.

– Day 4 –
How Shall We Rise?

Another of the old men questioned Amma Theodora, saying, "At the resurrection of the dead, how shall we rise?" She said, "As pledge, example, and prototype we have him who died for us and is risen, Christ our God."

The Sayings of the Desert Fathers, 84

Some Sundays ago a woman who, along with her husband, has been worshiping at my church for just a few months slipped a piece of paper into my hand moments before the service began. My mind was full of all that the next hour would involve—announcements, prayers, scripture, my sermon, and songs. I tucked the slip of paper into my pocket and promptly forgot about it—until about five days later, when I got a phone call from the woman, shyly wondering why I had not prayed in church according to her written request.

While talking with her I retrieved the paper from the pocket and was pained to see that it bore a prayer she had written on Sunday morning, when she had felt she would be unable to speak publicly in church. Her brother, whose nickname was Big Red, had died of lung cancer just hours before. She had wanted the congregation to give thanks for his life and to pray for his grieving family.

I promised her that I would lift up her prayer the very next Sunday, and apologized, embarrassed about my oversight. She mentioned that her family was Roman Catholic, and that a funeral Mass for her brother would be taking place at the parish church near her home in a small town about an hour's drive north of Tucson. I had preached a couple of times at the Presbyterian church in that town, and I knew the community had become economically depressed after the local copper mine had closed. I made an internal vow to attend the funeral Mass.

On a cool, sunny January afternoon in the high desert, I parked my car on the street in front of the modest brick church. I guessed it had been built in the 1950s, like all the surrounding, humble houses. Another car had just been parked by the curb in front of mine. Out of the backseat climbed a lanky man with longish, graying hair. He stood on the curb and unselfconsciously finished drinking the bottle of red wine he had apparently uncorked on the drive over. An elderly couple—his parents, perhaps—climbed gingerly out of the front seat, and the three of them made their way to the church's front steps, but didn't immediately enter the building.

Once inside the chilly sanctuary, I kept my jacket on. My two parishioners were standing close to one another near a front pew. He was wearing new Levis and a Western shirt. Her dark hair was smoothed into a bun and she wore a black dress. I greeted them and took a seat several pews back. The church walls bore wooden statues of saints, and the forced-air heater worked hard to warm the room. Little by little, family and friends arrived. One woman, whose hair was veiled in black lace, took snapshots of the gathered mourners. A toddler wore a little gray vest, and a man in a flannel shirt sat in the pew just ahead of mine, beside the man who had finished the wine.

"The last time I was in a Catholic church it was the Vatican. 1978," whispered the man in the flannel shirt. "The pope was as close to me as you are now."

"Close to the source," answered the other man.

"Real close."

Two wiry, auburn-haired women with fair, lined complex-ions entered the church and hugged everyone within reach. I remembered that my parishioner had told me her ancestors had been Spanish and Irish.

The priest was Nigerian, I guessed, and resplendent in white vestments. He talked with the family, making sure he knew Big Red's proper name, never having met him. Beside the altar stood a framed photo of Big Red, unsmiling, bearded, and wearing shades. The toddler rattled a rosary against a nearby pew. And then came the jangle of bells up the church's center aisle. As the sound grew louder behind me I wondered if this was some liturgical sign that the Mass was about to begin. But judging by the surprised expression on the priest's face, I knew it couldn't be. A man who looked to be six and a half feet tall, weighing little more than a hundred forty pounds, approached the altar, wearing long black jeans with a small brass cowbell, a chain and keys dangling from his belt. His head was wrapped in a dark blue bandanna, and his sunglasses didn't quite hide his blackened eyes. He spoke to the priest, then thanked him, and jangled to the very back pew.

I looked up at the pale, sagging crucifix hanging between the carved saints and was overcome by the feeling that it was precisely for these people that Jesus had lived and died. Once they all had made their ragged entrances, the Mass began. The priest spoke with a lilting accent about memories and love. Few people went forward to receive the Eucharist. After the priest had locked the host safely in the tabernacle, someone pressed a button on a portable CD player, and a sentimen-tal country song about eagles and tomorrow filled the room. As the song played on, the auburn-haired women held one another, kneeling and weeping in the front pew. One of the women waved her hand in the air, prayerfully telling Big Red good-bye.

I held my breath when she went to the pulpit to speak. I could not imagine what she could say, overcome with sorrow as she was. She whimpered a bit, but then found her voice:

"My brother was a good man. He was a fisherman. He was like a father to my kids, and he was one crazy mother-you-know-what-er. He loved life, and he loved us. He used to say—you remember—I love you like a racehorse loves to run. I love you like a racehorse loves to run."

"Sorry about the bell," said the man with the bandanna after he'd clanged his way to the pulpit. "Court ordered." People laughed weakly. He went on, "We had a lot of blood and mud and beer between us. Seemed like my brother and me could never have enough blood and mud and beer. And he loved my dogs. He would light *up*, man. He loved to load them into the back of my truck and ride out into the desert and watch the sunset or just watch the animals run. I was the one who couldn't handle it when he got cancer. He was all right. He said he was gonna live out his life, and he did. I'm the one who fell apart."

At first I'd thought this man's eyes had been blackened in a barroom fight. Now I knew they'd been bruised by grief. "At the resurrection of the dead," some old men once asked a Desert Mother named Amma Theodora, "how shall we rise?" It seemed to be just this question that had driven Big Red's friends and relations to church this afternoon. Maybe, I thought, Big Red's surviving brother would jangle out to his truck and drive deep into the desert with his dogs and a case of beer, to ask the sinking sun, *How the hell will we rise?* And maybe, after a long, unlit vigil, the sun would climb up again over the tops of the mountains, the snoozing dogs would stir awake, and Big Red's brother would know the answer to his question.

– Day 5 –
Whatever God Hands You

Abba Theodore of Enaton said, "When I was young, I lived in the desert. One day I went to the bakery to make two loaves, and there I found a brother also wanting to make bread, but there was no one to help him. So I put mine on one side, to lend him a hand. When the work was done, another brother came, and again I lent him a hand in cooking his food. Then a third came, and I did the same; and similarly one after the other, I baked for each of those who came. I made six batches. Later I made my own two loaves, since no one else came."

The Sayings of the Desert Fathers, 79

Look at your hands; give them a good, long look. They could tell you stories. They could tell other people stories about you.

When I see women with pretty manicures I sometimes envy their glossy fingernails. But I am rarely tempted to go get my own nails done because I think of my fingers as multipurpose tools that it would be impractical to decorate. I keep my fingernails clipped short and naked. They're not even as nice as the shiny nails on the infomercial guy who sells rolling cutters that can slice effortlessly through leather and glass. I don't want my fingernails to distract me from the task at hand; I don't want to hear them click on the computer keyboard as I write. I want to feel each letter as I type it. My husband Ken has pointed out to me that I don't need to type quite so aggressively. I think he worries that I will actually break the keyboard. Years ago I wrote stories at a manual typewriter, and that must be where I developed my heavy-handed ways.

Look at your hands. How well do you know the backs of them, the faint blue roadways of your veins, the tendons splayed like birds' feet under your skin, the knuckles, wrinkled like eyes in the bark of an aspen tree? Turn your hands over and consider your palms and your fingers, the thousand creases where you fold and hold onto things.

Remember the work of your hands. Where to begin? With your earliest efforts, the big, grown-up fingers your infant hand clutched? Do you remember the cool, vibrant slime of finger-paints? Everything you handled in those earliest days gave you a feel for the world, a good grasp.

Imagine the feel of handlebars, the grooved places you held as you rode your bike home from school. If you could get that old bike back, you would be amazed by its familiarity. Your fingers would remember where they once fit. Overall, though, the bike would feel small to you, and the world, for a moment, would seem larger than it does now, larger and far less damaged and scarred.

I have a scar on my wrist from the time I fell off my bike on the road near Bemis woods. I went down in the gravel. The scar is the faintest crescent in my skin. At first, when I looked for it just now, I couldn't find it, and that, to my surprise, made me sad. Wiping out on my bike is not a good memory. But it is *my* memory, and my scars are mine. I have grown attached to them over the years.

And your scars? The scars on your hands from that careless encounter with a paper cutter or an Exacto knife? The stories of how you came by your scars could tell things about you that nothing else could. I knew a woman who was born with only one hand. She wore a hook, wicked looking, but functional.

Still, nothing can do what five fingers can. She wrote whole books—philosophy treatises—single-handedly, but her hook couldn't hold steady a can of cat food. That's why she cut her hand badly one day with the edge of a can's pop-top lid. And they don't let one-handed people drive cars. She called a cab to carry her to the emergency room, her hand bound in a dish towel. The cat stayed home, contentedly lapping up pulverized ocean fish drizzled in human blood.

Think of the pets you have petted, the animals who have nosed and nudged at your hands, demanding affection, and getting it. Think of the people you have held, the babies, weighty and hot, the toddlers whose hands you insisted on holding in busy parking lots. Think of the kids who got too old to hold hands anymore, how they broke your heart before they got older still and became people who would actually take your hand in theirs once in a while, when life got too hard for them to get through with their hands just hanging there, useless and empty at their sides.

Your hands have spent their lives mostly full and occupied, not devilishly idle, not criminal, not usually. You know—I don't—if embedded anywhere within your fingers' unique, unrepeatable prints is some memory of wrongdoing. Don't tell me about it; tell God. And when you pray, don't lock your hands together like some unwelcoming church. Open your hands. Let go of their secrets and receive whatever God hands you, which at first may seem like nothing at all.

But it won't be nothing, this intangible blessing that will fall, weightless, into your upturned hands. It will be freedom. It won't cure the arthritis that has knotted your joints, and it won't fade the age spots that darken the thin skin between your knuckles and wrists. But it will be your freedom to do the good with your hands that you can do: lend a baker a hand kneading dough; knead tense shoulders; reassure your lover; write your book; applaud; comb your hair; wave hello.

- Day 6 -
I Deserve Better, Don't I?

[Amma Syncletica said], "Are you gold? You will pass through fire purged. Have you been given a thorn in the flesh? Exult, and see who else was treated like that . . . ."

The Forgotten Desert Mothers, 48

Once I sat in a circle of praying churchwomen. About a dozen of us had gathered in one woman's living room. She had let the bright wax of many candles drip from a shelf down a white plaster wall. She wore chartreuse sneakers with metallic leather trim and hugged people for several beats longer than they expected to be hugged. Her hugs were emphatic, counter-cultural. Her hugs said, *This is not an obligatory embrace; this is love, insistent and real.*

She did not seem sick, but she was. She had a huge, bawdy laugh and a disease that, I'd been told, was slowly hardening her flesh into bone. She had another, unrelated disease. "I'm a drunk," she would say. She'd been sober for close to twenty years. "I will always be a drunk."

Her spoken prayers were breathy and shocking. "Thank you, God, for making me sick. Thank you for my suffering."

When she said that, my eyes involuntarily snapped open and flashed a look her way. She sat cross-legged, swaying gently with her eyes closed, smiling like Buddha. She looked healthy and holy and crazy.

I will tell you right now, I am not thankful for my suffering. I hate my suffering, which, to date, has been pretty tame. I am not, to my knowledge, sick. My body works really quite well. My thick legs, which once inspired a man on the street to tell me I looked like a farm gal, get me around. My sinuses are good barometers; they tell me when it's going to rain. My skin holds me together, and my earlobes don't mind being pierced. God made me, and didn't do half bad, either. But when I suffer my mild ailments—when, for example, my cyclical hormones make a bloated misanthrope of me, a madwoman who seriously considers putting a bumper sticker on her car that says "As A Matter Of Fact, I *Do* Own The Road"—then I hate my suffering, and I indulge in the admittedly irrational but nevertheless compelling idea that I deserve better. I deserve a life without aches and mood fluctuations. Don't I?

Amma Syncletica, an ancient Desert Mother, says, *Nope.*

I say, Okay, what about cancer, which I don't have yet? Don't I deserve a life without cancer? I've prayed by the bedsides of people dying from cancer. I've officiated at their funerals. I've comforted their bereaved survivors. Shouldn't that make me somehow immune to catastrophic illness or mind-bending grief like theirs? Come on, work with me here.

I am working with you, says Amma Syncletica. *And I've got my work cut out for me.*

Syncletica, you said, "Have you been given a thorn in the flesh? Exult, and see who else was treated like that. . . ." But don't you think that's just a little—you know—*hairshirt?* I'm an American. We don't do suffering.

You just contradicted yourself, Amma says.

I say, What?

She says, *Americans do suffer. You suffer from a suffering disorder. That is, many of you deny your suffering, and when it becomes too intense to deny, you combat your suffering, which only worsens it. And that is disordered. You would do better to exult in your suffering, to give thanks for it, to learn its hard lessons.*

I say, You mean like that nutty woman with the bright green sneakers who hugs everyone for too long?

Yes, just like that exceptional woman. She is just sick and crazy and sober enough to admit that suffering, like the death she's waiting for, is not an aberration but a gift, albeit a difficult gift. You go sit at her green-sneakered feet. Like the diseases and sorrows you have somehow dodged thus far, she has much to teach you. And you have much to learn.

Amma Syncletica? I say.

Yes?

Learning is suffering.

How so?

Well, it hurts to gain new understanding. You have to admit your ignorance first, which isn't exactly our national pastime, we Americans. We're big on self-promotion around here.

You're big on hubris, you mean. You're big on the deadly sin of pride.

If you want to call it that. In any case, we are a commanding people. Humility, the stuff you have to summon if you're going to admit you're ignorant and learn anything, is for wimps.

Are you a wimp?

I am a wimp. I am an American wimp who can barely withstand her own PMS.

Now we're getting somewhere. Are you gold?

Am I gold?

Are you gold?

I would say I am an ore, an aggregate of minerals, some precious, some junk.

Some gold?

Okay, maybe some gold.

Very good. You are gold. You will pass through the fire purged. You will suffer. You will learn.

– Day 7 –
What Happened?

[Abba Poemen said], "Not understanding what has happened prevents us from going on to something better."

The Sayings of the Desert Fathers, 194

I love the church I serve as a pastor. I love the stalwarts who get there earlier than I do on Sunday mornings. I love the visitors who enter cautiously into worship, seeking a seat near the door. I love the covered patio, which, here in this desert, we call a ramada. I love the kids who giggle and pout during worship, who sell cookies during coffee hour and reap great revenues for their schools and scout troops. Early though it is in my ministry with this congregation, I have had days when my affection for its people has already been tempered and contoured—by fatigue, doubt, anxiety, annoyance, a pretty full range of the feelings that true love is roomy enough to include.

My present ministry is something much better than I experienced in previous ministries with two other churches. Now, let me emphasize: these two other congregations were lovely and faithful. God was in them and so were many fine souls who welcomed my pastoral efforts and remained appropriately oblivious to the tensions between their church's Senior Pastor and younger, Associate Pastor—me. I am generally too strong willed to be a happy Associate Pastor, and I love preaching too much not to do it most Sundays. So, my present ministry as a solo pastor who regularly preaches is the "something better" that Abba Poemen says we can only get to by "understanding what has happened."

What happened in these churches of my past?

What happened was this. When I was newly ordained to the ministry of Word and Sacrament, I served a congregation full of vibrant activists. The Senior Pastor was a folk hero. People revered him for his daring, prophetic work on behalf of the wretched of the earth. Pilgrims traveled great distances to hear him speak, to run their fingers through the waters of his church's baptismal font. His image once appeared on the front page of the Sunday newspaper, backlit, haloed by sunlight, iconic. He was one of the most brilliant orators I had ever heard. He would grumble and hiss and insist and reduce his antagonists to stammering nincompoops. You could feel your underarms burn when he really got going from the pulpit.

I didn't like him. I judged him, and I found him wanting. I spent a lot of time sitting beside him in his pickup truck, riding through the desert to meetings and funerals and the other places clergy go, and I noticed he was human, life-size, and flawed. Sometimes I felt bullied by him, and often professionally exploited. Once, at midnight on Christmas Eve, following a candlelit worship service, I was washing coffee cups in the church kitchen, and he ambled in. "All you need now," he remarked, "is to be barefoot and pregnant." I said nothing that night, but at other times I fought back, demanding respect that it may simply have been too late in life for him to learn to pay to a woman.

I began to feel soul-sick when I set foot on the church premises, which were beautiful, hewn of the soil, rocks, and lumber of the surrounding desert. The church doors bore iron handles shaped like the local reptiles. Rooted ocotillo fence posts sprouted green leaves and orangey blooms in the springtime. A cross big enough to crucify a man on stood in the prayer garden, and nothing about the church, which once had felt to me permeated by prayer and Spirit the way terra-cotta can be permeated by cool water, could heal my soul-sickness. I fought on, though. I argued with my elder colleague and I vilified him sometimes and defended myself and ultimately wept and then finally walked out for good, my thoughts warped and shimmering like a mirage, my gut feeling kicked in by a frightened man wearing pointed boots.

Now I needed a job. Incurable church lady that I was, I wound up in another church three weeks later, working for a showman, a wannabe-Bono bully-pulpit preacher who had nothing good to say about his mother, his ex-wife, or the last clergywoman he'd fired. I had not yet met Abba Poemen or considered the meaning of his words, "Not understanding what has happened prevents us from going on to something better."

For a few months into this second ministry, I didn't understand. How could I have found another jerk to work for so fast?

This was a silly question. Aggressive, territorial, insecure, uncollegial clergy are a dime a dozen. The church, after all, is a haven for sinners, and generally a good boss is hard to find. Also hard to come by is understanding—understanding of what has happened, a clear and courageous retrospective grasp of things, including one's own compulsions and errors and knack for reproducing old traumas.

In my quest for understanding I enlisted the help of a minister, a petite and compassionate woman who burned incense, fed me elderberry lozenges, referred to God as "Holy Mystery," and listened to me long and well. How is it that being understood brings understanding? This may be one of our holiest mysteries. All I know is that after numerous months, by the time my kind listener moved away from this desert and I could talk with her no longer, I no longer needed to talk with her. I had attained a grain of understanding. I had even managed to muster a measure of compassion for the clergymen in whose churches I had not been fully free to flourish.

And so I find myself in another church, in another haven for sinners among whom, for all we know, I am the chief example of human fallibility. And yet, here I need not fight for respect, and this is something better, much better, than I experienced working for pastors who seemed afraid to be outshone by a female subordinate. Here I am pastor to people who, now and then, fatigue and annoy me, who very occasionally behave so badly they make me doubt the wisdom of my ever having become a church lady, people who elevate my anxieties at times, people who lift my heart even higher than my anxieties, people of God, every one of them, people I love, every one of them.

– Day 8 –
Little Lady

Another time, two old men, great anchorites, came to the district of Pelusia to visit [Amma Sarah]. When they arrived, one said to the other, "Let us humiliate this old woman." So they said to her, "Be careful not to become conceited thinking to yourself: 'Look how anchorites are coming to see me, a mere woman.'" But Amma Sarah said to them, "According to nature, I am a woman, but not according to my thoughts."

The Forgotten Desert Mothers, 38–39

The man who mistrusts me, who tests and insults me—
does he aim to see me fail?
Would he enjoy watching me flail
and thrash and finally succumb
to the dumb, girlish foibles he supposes define me?
I must be mad
to suspect he secretly respects me,
or at least hopes to see me exceed
his low expectations and elude his aggression.
But wouldn't he be disappointed to destroy me?
His victory would be the saddest sort of gain.

25

There I'd be, felled at close range
by bullets only lame prey couldn't dodge,
and that would make him less a sharp shooter
than a taker of cheap shots. I am not
his enemy, though he tempts me repeatedly
to turn against him. What sorrow
does his grimace hide? Tomorrow
he may menace me. Today
all I see is a decent man in pain,
unable to vanquish his own frailties,
reflexively jabbing at mine.
That's fine. The God we both worship,
possessed of countless gracious wiles,
is powerful to save and bound to reconcile
even this little lady and that tough guy.

- Day 9 -
To Blame Myself

Theophilus of holy memory, the bishop of Alexandria, once went to the mount of Nitria, and a hermit of Nitria came to see him. The bishop said, "What have you discovered in your life, abba? The hermit answered, "To blame myself unceasingly." The bishop said, "That is the only way to follow."

The Desert Fathers, 154

One day, as I sat composing a sermon in my church office, a capable and dedicated member of the church—moderator of an important and active church committee—telephoned me. With obvious tension in her voice, she said, "I was upset after yesterday's meeting."

I felt a little hiccup in my heart and blurted, "Uh-oh." Then I collected myself and added, "Do you want to talk about why?"

"Can I come by your office?"

We agreed on a time to meet. After we hung up, I began to worry and speculate about what I had done to upset this vital and good-natured lay leader. It didn't take me long to arrive at a theory about just how I had encroached on her territory and failed to live up to my own ideals of collegiality. I had invited a newer member of the church to join the committee, but had

27

neglected first to check this out with the committee moderator, who, I guessed, had been caught off guard by the newcomer's presence, and as a result may have felt I had undermined or even disrespected her. I squirmed internally, feeling my imperfection. I wished I had been impeccable.

Never far from my awareness are my memories of working for pastors who could rarely admit to a mistake or apologize for it. These elder colleagues taught me a great deal about hubris and stubbornness, a forceful combination of traits effective for maintaining domination over others. Tyranny is easier than collaboration—for the tyrant. Much as I believe in democratic church leadership, I practice democracy imperfectly, especially when I'm tempted to use my power to get my way, if only to save time or to arrive at a decision I believe is the right one for everyone.

Doubtless I could and should have consulted the now-upset committee moderator before inviting a newcomer to her committee. Mentally I prepared my apology and hoped she would accept it. Simultaneously, I cooked up little defenses. The newcomer's participation in the committee meeting had been helpful, hadn't it? Wasn't that really the point? But this self-protective angle didn't sit well with me, so I did my best to overcome my pride, and finished composing my sermon.

At the appointed time the committee moderator arrived at my office. Her hands moved about in abrupt and agitated gestures, and her usually untroubled face looked as grim as I had ever seen it. And then she began to apologize. She catalogued for me the failings she perceived in herself, while also affirming that she felt God had called her to her leadership role in the church.

"But I'll certainly leave the committee," she said, "if that's what you need me to do. I just don't know who'd replace me. For now, I'm afraid I'm all you've got."

A strange combination of feelings welled up within me. I felt relief and compassion at the same time—relief, in a primal, childlike way, that this woman wasn't angry at *me*, and compassion for her as she struggled with her self-directed anger.

As it turned out, she had not been upset by the presence of the newcomer at the meeting. She'd been upset with herself for having run the meeting imperfectly, which, she feared, had given the newcomer a terrible first impression. For the hurting woman sitting with me, the final analysis was: *It's all my fault.* Little did she know that I, too, had entered into our conversation prepared to accept blame for her unhappiness.

According to Theophilus of holy memory and an unnamed hermit with whom he conferred, we were both right, which is to say, we were both wrong, both guilty. "To blame myself unceasingly" was, for the hermit and for Theophilus, the only path to righteousness.

But imagine if I had said to the anxious and fine-hearted woman in my office, "Yes, it *is* your fault. You are, in fact, inadequate, but by realizing this, you draw closer to God."

Of course there are pastors who, historically, have said roughly this to their parishioners. I am sure some still promote theologies of God's sovereignty by emphasizing human depravity in the most degrading terms. I have known more than one preacher who reveled in shaming his congregation. In those moments I expect the worshipers learned much more about their psychologically wounded, overcompensating pastor than they learned about their loving and merciful God.

All pastors work from the vantage point of our own souls, consciously or not, constructively or not. I try to be conscious and constructive, and to share with parishioners glimpses of my own fixer-upper of a soul when I believe doing so might help them to know they are not unique or alone in their struggles, that even "religious professionals" have plenty of foibles to contend with.

So I told the nervous, tearful woman in my office about my latest administrative fumble. As I'd imagined she would do, she brushed it off as nothing. And I said, "See! That's how I look at the 'mistakes' that are looming so large in *your* mind."

And God? How does God view our self-doubt and self-blame?

"To blame myself unceasingly" may have seemed a worthy aspiration to some ancient desert monastics, but it is not for you, not for me, and not for the troubled woman who came to see me in my office. This doesn't mean we can't learn from Theophilus of holy memory and the other hermits of the ancient Near East. It means that by modern standards of emotional and spiritual health, some desert ascetics took humility too far, made humiliation of it, and valorized it to boot. The dangers inherent in such a move cannot be overemphasized.

A friend of mine is just now painfully extracting herself from a humiliating marriage. Her spouse's unrelenting belittlements implied, day by degrading day, that only by believing in her supposed unworthiness could my friend receive the emotional abuse that had come to pass for love in their home. As she renovates her life in the cramped apartment where she now lives alone, my friend acknowledges her partial responsibility for the disaster her marriage became.

"I accepted the abuse," she tells me over the phone.

She did accept the abuse, and coming to understand why will help her never again to put up with it. But accepting responsibility for her choices will not be the same as self-blame, which would only seem to confirm that abuse is what she deserved.

What she deserves, what you and I and the woman who came to my office deserve, is love, undisguised and unconditional—not because we have earned love by our perfectionism, but because we live in the kingdom of God, and here the old rules no longer apply. Here in the kingdom of God we can make mistakes great and small, but we can't unmake our redemption. Errors, flaws, foibles, fumbles and all, we are—by God—made good.

– Day 10 –
Wherever I Go I Find Support

A brother said to Abba Poemen, "I see that wherever I go I find support." The old man said to him, "Even those who hold a sword in their hands have God who takes pity on them in the present time. If we are courageous, he will have mercy on us."

The Sayings of the Desert Fathers, 180

Years ago I cashiered at a store called Bob's, which sold over three thousand periodicals and maybe thirty brands of cigarettes. Occasionally a blue-eyed French woman would come in to buy Marlboros and a newspaper. Once a coworker of mine asked her a question to which she responded with an uncomprehending look and the heavily accented answer, "All I know is Sugar Blue."

Sugar Blue was the woman's boyfriend, a musician the Rolling Stones had "discovered" playing his harmonica on the streets of Paris. They had hired him to play a bluesy riff and a solo on their song "Miss You." Now Sugar Blue had gone from performing for a few spare francs to being a "harp hero," headlining at the Kingston Mines in Chicago. Now Sugar Blue's girlfriend, who understood more English than she spoke, found herself in the middle of America, picking up packs of smokes and slightly outdated issues of *Le Monde* at Bob's.

Once in a while, when I feel far out of my element and reluctant to adapt to life as it is, her words come back to me, dreamy and defensive. *All I know is Sugar Blue.*

I maintained such a state of mind for months after my husband Ken and I moved from Chicago to Tucson. It was August in the Sonoran Desert, and when monsoon rains weren't drenching the land and flooding the arroyos, the sky, unmarked and burning, seemed to me intent on obliterating all subtlety and variation from the earth. I felt I had to hurry from my car to the grocery store lest I melt into the parking lot's asphalt like a ribbon of tar. In the produce section, artificial rains from snaking hoses misted the vegetables to keep them fresh, and other shoppers, stranger strangers than the ones "back home," selected mangoes and jicama. Feeling as forsaken as Mick Jagger moaning, "Lord, I miss you," I longed for the elm trees that flanked and shaded the residential streets in my lost, humid city. Chicago stood, far away, tall and industrious beside a great, juicy lake it seemed I would never see again.

In our new, rented home, I would sit at the desk I had painted a glossy aquamarine and wish I could dive back into my foregone life. One day, in desperation and despair, I pressed the heels of my hands against my shut eyes and pleaded, "God, help me. Come *on*. Show me a sign."

An image came into my awareness, the face of a woman I had met at the church where Ken and I had worshiped a handful of times since moving to Tucson. The woman's name was Jean, and she was my mother's age. After a long illness, her husband had died, just weeks before I had met her. I scarcely knew Jean yet, but I had her phone number, so I swallowed once and called.

"I know this will sound a little weird, and I don't tend to do this sort of thing, but I was praying and I think I'm being led to you, somehow."

In what I have come to know and love as Jean's customary, matter-of-fact way of living, she welcomed me into her life then and there. She refers to herself as "Mama Jean," and she is certainly to me a desert *amma*, a confidante who "gives me a word," who encourages me and kindly calls me on my nonsense when I need her to.

Jean has resided in Tucson for a decade or more, but during her marriage to an international construction contractor she lived as "a potted plant," establishing and maintaining households wherever her husband's job took the family, adapting to life in places as far-flung as Little Rock, Arkansas and Saudi Arabia.

In the latter desert Jean learned to "eat like you'll never see another meal and drink like you'll never see another toilet." Now, desert dwellers understand that staying hydrated is crucial, and many Southwesterners carry bottled water wherever we go. But few people in my life possess Jean's adaptability, her make-it-work horse sense and survival skills. God surely brought her face to my anguished, praying mind's eye that day, when all I knew was Sugar Blue, because Jean is what I most needed: an icon of practicality and calm, an embodiment of down-to-earth hope, a friend.

"I see," a brother said to the Desert Father Abba Poemen, "that wherever I go I find support." Saudi Arabia and Little Rock, Arkansas taught Jean to see, as this brother saw, that God precedes and follows us always and everywhere, providing the mercy and support we need.

Summoning the courage to accept and be transformed by God's provisions is our challenge. By faith, we can rise to it. The other option is to stay dreamy and defensive, knowing only Sugar Blue, singing only, "Lord, I miss you," or, like the exiled Israelites in Babylon, hanging our harps in the weeping willows and refusing to sing at all. If we do that, we might miss out on meeting the likes of Mama Jean. Who, then, will help us make it work? Who will teach us to sing to the Lord a new song?

– Day 11 –
Door-to-Door Penitence

Amma Sarah said, "If I prayed God that all people should approve of my conduct, I should find myself a penitent at the door of each one, but I shall rather pray that my heart may be pure toward all."

The Forgotten Desert Mothers, 39

It's Saturday, and I'm one for one. This week I've made one apology and accepted one apology. My little world is in balance. I can cross both "repent" and "forgive" off my to-do list.

Well, maybe not.

Chances are, tomorrow I will overlook a dear soul, or speak carelessly, or fail to fulfill an obligation, you name it, and "repent" will have to go right back on my list. To say nothing of the little offenses I might suffer: his sarcasm, her bossiness.

We're never finished, are we? We've never said "I'm sorry" once and for all.

But that makes it sound so burdensome and perpetual, like the task of the mythic Sisyphus, rolling his boulder forever uphill, never getting to the top, never giving it a rest.

My husband Ken knows a man I will call Sisyphus, who's perennially sorry because he's perennially offensive. Sisyphus is an elder colleague of Ken's. He served on the search committee that years ago hired Ken to teach on the faculty of a major university. During Ken's grueling, weekend-long job interview, he suffered a head cold so severe he had to keep discreetly dosing himself with over-the-counter decongestants and pain relievers. He picked at his entrées in fancy restaurants where the interrogations stretched late into the evenings.

"What theorists have influenced your work?" asked Sisyphus. For an academic like Ken, this is a big question. He laid down his fork and began to answer, but Sisyphus couldn't stick around to listen. He had to run to the bar for a smoke and another cognac.

At the end of the evening, once he was back at the table, Sisyphus noticed Ken's barely-touched salmon. "Are you going to finish that?" he asked.

Ken felt the throbbing ache in his sinuses and answered, "Um, no. Why?"

"I'll take it," Sisyphus said, reaching over to scrape Ken's leftovers into his own to-go container.

"To your health," Ken said in disbelief.

Once he had joined the faculty, Ken observed that Sisyphus often behaved this impulsively. He spoke with such aggressive conviction during meetings that his colleagues occasionally fled in tears.

"I'm a bull in a china shop, I know," said Sisyphus. "I'm sorry."

"I'm sorry," he said, again and again. But he never actually changed his behavior. It seemed as though he wasn't sorry at all.

Not long after Ken had received tenure, Sisyphus asked him out to lunch. Once they were seated at the restaurant, Sisyphus said he had already eaten. While Ken chewed on his sandwich, Sisyphus accused him of failing to pull his weight in the department. "Maybe we shouldn't have granted you tenure," said Sisyphus.

Ken is a rhetorician. He studies and teaches the ancient arts of argumentation. He practiced these arts just then, with a cool, systematic ferocity that could have made Aristotle blush.

Sisyphus might have slunk away from the table, had it not been for the invisible boulder in his lap, comprised, I suspect, of his own colossal shame and compensatory arrogance.

"I'm sorry," Sisyphus later told Ken. "I'm a bull in a china shop, I know." And then he did it all again to somebody else: the insults, the apologies. And he did it yet again.

"If I prayed God that all people should approve of my conduct," said Amma Sarah, "I should find myself a penitent at the door of each one." You can't please all the people, Sarah seems to be telling us. Try to, and you'll become nothing more than a door-to-door penitent.

Or, like Sisyphus, offend all the people and achieve the same result.

Either way, it's a sorry way to live.

The way to live with other human beings, Sarah says, is with a purified heart that presumes no one guilty until proven innocent; a heart that turns to God that it might not turn on others; a heart cleaner, wider open, more forbearing and forgiving than is my own heart toward the man I call Sisyphus, who hurt my husband, and thus hurt me, too.

"Create in me a clean heart, O God, and put a new and right spirit within me" (Psalm 51:10). Surely this was Sarah's prayer when she wasn't asking Christ to intercede on behalf of all people, including those who disapproved of her.

If I prayed God that all people should approve of my conduct, my prayer—*please let them like me*—would resemble my anxious ruminations when I was thirteen years old and starting to attend a new middle school. For adolescents, *please let them like me* is a suitable interior plea. But mature Christians—among whom Amma Sarah is exemplary—manage to want more than this. Or, to put it another way, mature Christians manage to want less for themselves than they want for others. It was not for her own sake that Amma Sarah desired a purified heart, but for the sake of those who had to deal with her.

Apparently they liked her. Much more than this, the people who had the good fortune to know Amma Sarah clearly revered her, learned from her, remembered what she said. Had she been a lousy neighbor, a repeat offender, and a door-to-door penitent who never really changed, Sarah would long ago have been forgotten. But here I sit on a Saturday early in the twenty-first century, thinking back over my week with its balance of repentance and forgiveness, and this ancient, wizened woman of the desert teaches me to lay aside my tallies, to pray simply to receive a new and right spirit—for the good of everybody, including myself, Sisyphus, my beloved husband Ken, strangers, parishioners, friends, and people who approve neither of my conduct nor of me.

– Day 12 –

Saying Nothing

At a meeting of monks in Scetis, the hermits wanted to test Moses. So they poured scorn on him, saying, "Who is this black man who is here with us?" . . . When the meeting had dispersed, the monks who had insulted him asked him, "Weren't you upset inside?" He replied, "I was upset, and I said nothing."

The Desert Fathers, 173

Years ago my husband Ken and I were to be guests at a small wedding in central Florida. The rehearsal dinner, a barbecue, took place the night before at a remote hunting lodge. As happens on such occasions, we found ourselves spending hours with people we would never otherwise have met. I think especially of the bridegroom's cousin, Carl, who lived somewhere near the lodge. After the wedding party had eaten our fill of ribs, potato salad, and pecan pie, and the parents of the bride and groom were chatting over sweet tea, Carl addressed the young adults.

"You crackers wanna see some gators?"

Seven or eight of us out-of-towners glanced at one another. I'd never heard the term "cracker" before, much less been addressed as one. I hesitated, fingering the gummy varnish on the dinner table, and then thought, *What the hell. When in Rome.*

With the others, I followed Carl out into the damp, chirping night. Darkness now obscured the huge live oak trees draped with Spanish moss that we'd passed on the long, beautiful-but-creepy drive to the lodge. On the way in, unaccustomed as Ken and I were to subtropical forests, we'd half-joked about never getting out of there alive.

Carl had a flashlight and a local's surefootedness. I took Ken's hand. We cautious, clustered guests, none of us dressed for a hike, followed Carl's faint silhouette and the wavering, luminous circle that preceded him. We fell quiet, concentrating on our footsteps. Carl led us down a forest path canopied by tree limbs that we couldn't see but knew were there because we couldn't see the moon or stars, either. Eventually we could see the sky, black with a generous scattering of bright eyelets and a washed-out, lopsided moon. We ventured onto soil so wet it nearly sucked off our shoes, then filed down a jetty that extended to the center of a marsh. A burping chorus of frogs surrounded us. Carl snapped off his flashlight and let our eyes adjust to the steamy moonlight on the water, which looked viscous and murky as sorghum.

We watched the surface of the water for bulges that might be alligators' heads. When the bride-to-be bent and dipped her hand into the water, her brother warned her, "Careful. You don't want to wind up alligator bait."

"That's all right," Carl drawled. "They only like dark meat."

And so here it was, the ugly, inescapable cliché of the Deep Southern racist. And there were the rest of us, educated white liberal Northerners, appalled into speechlessness, lined up on a boardwalk overhanging a swamp. To this day I regret my dumb nonresponse to Carl. Once his words had made their sickening impact on me, once the shock had subsided and the frogs no longer seemed to be chanting hateful slurs, I was able to formulate articulate objections in my brain, but I spoke none of them, and everybody else stayed silent, too. Then someone faked a yawn or tapped the face of a glowing wristwatch or made a crack about needing beauty sleep or said whatever it is embarrassed cowards say when it's time to slither home from a supremely awkward evening. I can't help imagining the submerged, unseen alligators smiled when we human beings turned around to leave.

Those who have studied the place and time called "Late Antique Egypt," in which many Desert Christians lived, generally agree that black people in the ancient world did not suffer from systematic racial discrimination like that which African Americans still face. The late Howard University classicist, Frank Snowden, wrote, "in science, philosophy and religion color was not the basis of a widely accepted theory concerning the inferiority of blacks."[3] But before contemporary readers too readily conclude that fourth-century monks offer an ancient alternative to modern prejudices, we need to grapple with the story of a desert monk named Moses, whose own monastic brothers "poured scorn on him, saying, 'Who is this black man who is here with us?'" Doesn't Moses' story illustrate early Christians' overt discrimination against African-descended people?

Dubiously, one present-day promoter of the Desert Christians says no. She is the anonymous blogger of "Daily Desert Wisdom." Under the avatar "Amma Syncletica," she posts on the World Wide Web "a daily drop of wisdom from the men and women who turned to the desert for spiritual testing and transformation on their journey toward God." In a post entitled "The Patience of Moses" she writes: "Moses was a black man from Ethiopia who was often teased about the color of his skin. He accepted such humor happily, aware of the affection with which it was offered."[4]

"Amma Syncletica" overlooks the explicit content of the story about Moses, in which he says in response to the brothers who "poured scorn on him," "I was upset, and I said nothing." Her portrayal of Moses' silence as patient, happy acceptance of the monks' supposedly affectionate humor denies and rationalizes obvious ethnic discrimination and the pain it causes in any era. The blogger's syrupy misrepresentation of Moses' silence publicly manifests the same present-day unwillingness to confront racism by which we suddenly mute wedding guests tacitly endorsed Carl's repulsive remark at the alligator swamp. Much as readers of early Christian literature may wish to believe the scholar Frank Snowden's assertion that the ancient world was free of white supremacist ideology, we are nevertheless obliged to interrogate critically such troubling realities as "the prevalence of dark-skinned demons and temptresses in the visions of the desert fathers."[5]

In some stories about Abba Moses his skin color goes unmentioned and he simply exemplifies monastic humility and the wisdom of a spiritual master. But then there is this account:

> It was said of Abba Moses that he was ordained and the ephod placed upon him. The archbishop said to him, "See, Abba Moses, now you are entirely white." [Moses] said to him, "It is true of the outside, lord and father, but what about Him who sees the inside? . . . So [Moses] came in and they covered him with abuse, and drove him out, saying, "Outside, black man!" Going out he said to himself, "They have acted rightly concerning you, for your skin is as black as ashes. You are not a man, so why should you be allowed to meet men?"

The desert fathers and mothers may have envisioned evil spirits as dark-skinned beings, but the real evil was and is prejudice more profound than skin deep, with power to make its victims hate themselves. The demon of racism, as Carl reminded the rest of us "crackers," has yet to be exorcised from the human heart.

– Day 13 –
Iona Stone

They said of Agatho that for three years he kept a stone in his mouth in order to teach himself silence.

The Desert Fathers, 20

From the slender black cord around my neck hangs an Iona stone. It is a smooth rock, roughly the dimensions of a gigante bean. An artisan who lives on the Isle of Iona, off the west coast of Scotland, scavenged the stone at low tide and put it through a tumbler with comparable finds until it emerged, full-color and polished. I think of it as a map of the Hebridean seascape. There, just beneath the gray, pearlescent sky, undulant with changes, the North Atlantic lies cold but restless and reflective, inlaid with islands. My pale stone pendant, blotched mineral-green, graphs these latitudes, its own origins.

Because I am a Christian, a believer in fantastic, sacred stories, my Iona stone, for which I paid £6 in an island gift shop, is meaningful to me, full of meaning. Floating near its tiny images of overcast islands I see a brown speck, St. Columba's creaking, hide-and-wicker coracle, laden with a cargo of a dozen brave evangelists. I lay the stone like a lozenge on my tongue, half expecting it still to taste of sea salt, but it's as neutral as my teeth, only cooler. If I were to suck it as the sea sucks the edges of Iona, the stone, like Iona, would take forever to dissolve. Even Iona's ancient abbey, once ruined by abandonment and centuries and weather, lasted. The stone church waited like a bone to be resurrected, enfleshed.

And it was, from within. The Iona community, ecumenical, simple, just and liturgical, was born in the twentieth century and comprises the island's human heart. Sunday mornings, passenger ferries arrive at the dock. Pilgrims wearing mackintoshes and Wellingtons pour out of boats and hurry uphill to church, oblivious, it seems, to the harangue of ravens in the isle's tallest trees, or to the local lambs, bleating and hustling away from the rapid crunch of rubber boot soles on gravel. The humans hurry to worship, to consider the ravens, to bless the Lamb of God who takes away the sin of the world.

Put a stone in your shoe, a writing teacher once advised a young poet. It will heighten your awareness, make you take notice. Put a stone in your mouth, a monk once told himself. It will shut you up for three years. Hang a stone on a string around your neck, a Celtic shopkeeper once advised her customer. It will show you the way back to Iona, this patch of briny desert. Here, when winter comes, with its penetrating, horizontal rains and infrequent ferries, you could contemplate cartographies of silence and prayer. You could walk the island's edges and discover your life, how like a stone on a shoreline it is: created and accounted for, smaller than it once was and shrinking imperceptibly, tumbling into beauty, taking part in forever, taking part of forever to dissolve into God.

– Day 14 –
Love, Tomorrow, Nevertheless

The holy Bishop Epiphanius related that some crows, flying all around the temple in the presence of blessed Athanasius, cried without interruption, "Caw, caw." Then some pagans, standing in front of blessed Athanasius, cried out, "Wicked old man, tell us what these crows are crying." He answered, "These crows are saying, 'Caw, caw,' and in the Ausonion (or Latin) language, this word means 'tomorrow.'"

The Sayings of the Desert Fathers, 56

My husband and I lived in a crow's nest in the city, it seemed. We lived among elm trees, generations old, rooted between sidewalks and parked cars, their highest branches outreaching even our third-floor apartment. Crows made their nests among the elm branches. In our living room a screen door that once had led to a breezy sleeping porch now led to nothing but the air outside, noisy with urban crowing, the porch having been ruined by elements, exhaust fumes, and time, and eventually demolished. At a table in the living room, beside that screen door, amid cacophonous birdsong and the occasional blare of sirens from the streets below, I wrote a poem called "Consider the Ravens," in which blackbirds cried "God, God, God." How was I to know they were actually crying "tomorrow"?

I might have figured it out, had today been less compelling. The present was heady. I spent much of it in a deliciously pulpy-smelling library full of books about God. One book in particular, written in Greek, took me weeks to decipher, and then I found the meaning dull. "God is love," the book said. And again, "God is love." I dared to wonder, so what if God is love? The message, simplistic, monosyllabic, seemed unworthy of the effort I had put into extracting it. Little did I know how badly I would need to know that God is love, tomorrow. I simply turned my attention to the day at hand, with its sufficient evils and demands, its tough, hungry crows, nesting and crying near my windows. "Tomorrow," they called, but I thought I heard "God."

I thought I heard God in the screech of elevated train brakes and in the carbon monoxide–scented winds that blew down the city's architectural canyons. I thought I saw God's shroud in the cloud cover overhead, and sensed the workmanlike hand of God moving amid industrial and residential neighborhoods alike. I had lived in the city for so long that its machinations were the only incarnations of the holy I knew—dangerous and unbeautiful though the place surely looked to outsiders. I was an insider, familiar with the metropolitan grid and pace, its map and rhythms imprinted so deeply in my mind that rush-hour traffic seemed downright liturgical. A place to park my car? That was an answer to prayer.

Which is to say I had not much of a prayer life, although I did a lot of vague, mystical longing in that city, and rarely skipped church. But I was too small-minded, despite what I fancied to be my urbanity, to know yet what it really is to pray. To pray is gladly to put oneself at the mercy of a God who will not disclose what tomorrow may hold. Much prayer deals in fear and asks God to be merciful, to make tomorrow better than, or at least as good as, today. God already is merciful; that request is needless. But God's mercy tends not to issue in the progressive improvement of our personal circumstances. Things do not just keep getting better for you and me. And yet God is merciful—indeed, God is love. To pray is to be loved, despite our small-mindedness and our big fears.

I went, one year, from a contented, small-minded sense that this was all there ever would be, this city life of books and poetry, of elevated trains and God and me, to big fear of the American desert, the sunshiny sprawl of it all, pocked here and there by housing developments and strip malls. We were called to move to this desert by the same God I had long believed in, who was now behaving unrecognizably, demanding trust I could not come up with, providing far less assurance than I felt I required. This was neither the tomorrow I had wanted nor a today I believed I could work with. In our strange new desert home every theological thought I had ever considered seemed as useless as an ancient Greek book telling me God is love or urging me to consider the ravens, how they neither sow nor reap and yet God feeds them.

There were no crows in our new desert, no ravens to consider, no old city streets flanked and shaded by elms in which crows could have nested, no screen door that opened to a sky full of birds squawking God's name or siren shrieks rising up from the earth. The desert was all dirt and dearth, its landscape all garishly sunlit, sun-bleached, sunburned.

I wandered in a spiritual wilderness so archetypal I felt my life was being conceived by a screenwriter who had undergone Jungian analysis. I developed a prayer life in the desert, which is to say I did a lot of devotional bitching. I prayed like a psalmist, lamenting until I was all complained out, and the only word left to say was *nevertheless*.

I tried to say *no*, but it came out *tomorrow*. And then I said *God*, but it sounded like *love* and it felt like mercy—not Hollywood mercy (which I would have preferred), not mercy that douses the fire and saves you in the nick of time, but mercy that lets you burn and burns with you and then salves your wounds and stays by your side while you slowly heal and become someone scarred and grateful, deeply different from the blithe and lucky kid you used to be.

– Day 15 –

Not the End of the Word

A hermit said, "The prophets wrote books. Our predecessors came after them, and then their successors memorized them. But this generation copies them onto papyrus and parchment and leaves them unused on the window ledge."

The Desert Fathers, 117

A philosopher or two, a handful of nihilists, and then a glossy news magazine to which millions of Americans subscribed proclaimed all at once: "God is dead." Now, a few decades later, a dozen professional believers in God, pastors who also were writers, presented themselves at a workshop entitled "Writing and the Pastoral Life." It took place at a conference center affiliated with a Benedictine monastery and university. The conferees, of whom I was one, sat around a table nodding appreciatively as one of our kind insisted: "The Word is not dead."

The Word's obituary, like that of God, had been published prematurely. The Word, some observers of popular culture had recently announced, had been replaced by the image. Video could do what no written language could, and nobody knew this better than the young, the watchers of YouTube and inhabitants of MySpace. Although they had been born decades after the "God is Dead" scare, America's youth were living, some

members of the conferees' churches feared, as if God had in fact
died, to be succeeded by Bono, Jon Stewart, and Brangelina.

Church folk who worry about idolatry among their progeny
tend also to worry about biblical literacy—their own and their
children's and their children's children's. *Should they really be
watching VeggieTales during Sunday School? Why don't more of them
sign up for Vacation Bible School? Do they even know the Lord's Prayer?
And by the way, where's the pastor? Why isn't she in her office?*

I wasn't in my church office because I was enjoying a remarkable privilege called Pastoral Study Leave. I was away,
whole states and climates away from my church, talking with
kindred spirits about writing and pastoral life, or what I had
come to think of as, well, ministry of the Word. When I wasn't
listening or talking I was writing words or reading them, in a
narrow room, a modern monastic cell.

I read the words of a third-century desert hermit: "The
prophets wrote books. Our predecessors came after them, and
then their successors memorized them. But this generation copies them onto papyrus and parchment and leaves them unused
on the window ledge." This old curmudgeon sounded a lot like
some church elders I had worked with. Furthermore, the hermit's gripe was echoed in a story told by the luminary in our
midst, a renowned, prolific author at whose feet we conferees
had gathered to learn. He had paraphrased the entire Bible into
accessible, everyday speech, and huge segments of the Christian
public had embraced his earthy, energetic rendering of scripture.
An 87-year-old woman had written him a fan letter of sorts.

"She had twenty-one nieces and nephews," said the author,
"and not one of them reads the Bible. She heard about my
paraphrase and bought herself a copy, to check key passages
alongside the King James Version. My version passed. So she
went and bought twenty-one more copies of it, to give to her
nieces and nephews. But at the end of her letter she wrote,
'P.S. I still read the King James.'"

It's never too early or too late to get nostalgic for that old-
time religion. But actually the die-hard King James Bible fan

displayed a more progressive attitude than do some tradition-
alists I know who still refer to a hymnal published in 1989 as
"new." To them, a contemporary paraphrase of scripture is as
papyrus and parchment scrolls were to the cranky third-century
hermit: trendy and decadent—a death knell, if not for God,
then for the Word as we knew it.

We conferees took a break from talking, reading, writing,
and eating to pray vespers with the local monks. In an aggressively modern church, all poured concrete and geometric
windows, we chanted ancient Hebrew psalms translated into a
dignified, muscular English. After the benediction, a monk who
had prayed and worked there since 1949 granted our group a
tour of the church, including its rarely-seen relic room.

On stony shelves, curvaceous, shining reliquaries held the
purported femurs and eyeballs of great or little-known saints.
Most remarkable of all was the saint in the floor, a whole skeleton supine in a sunken glass-and-concrete crypt, its bone feet
shod in sequined slippers, its skull swathed in what looked to
be silk chiffon. The saint seemed to have lain down and died
in a prom dress a few generations earlier, but was said to have
been exhumed from the Roman catacombs. This would have
made the skeleton even older than the desert hermit who had
complained about those newfangled parchment scrolls. "I used
to teach physics," said our group's monastic tour guide, point-
ing toward the encrypted skeleton. "I'm seeking permission to
have him carbon dated."

At what point does innovation obliterate tradition? When
does newness render unrecognizable or prove counterfeit the
books and bones our forebears bequeathed to us? And once
we dismantle or debunk the past, with its antiquated practices
and artifacts, how are we to believe in the God to whom these
heirlooms once pointed? What language shall we borrow, and
from what place or century, to give words to the One we dare
to hope can never die?

The next evening we conferees visited with a book editor
who hinted at some answers. An approachable ex-Franciscan

friar, he was newly working for a press that had been involved in publishing the revolutionary vernacular liturgies that followed Vatican II. But now, even as the editor watched many leaders of his church backpedaling from theological and linguistic advancements made in the mid-twentieth century, he kept looking forward to receiving fresh manuscripts written in languages both respectful of religious history and reflective of present realities. He maintained this hope despite grim developments he enumerated for our gathered group of pastor-writers: the near-elimination of independent bookstores from the American landscape, the ever-decreasing numbers of readers, the expanding quantities of slick, insubstantial books hyped each year.

In near disbelief, one of the conferees said: "Let me get this straight. Nobody reads anymore, but more books than ever are being published." These words bluntly paraphrased yet once more the saying of that desert hermit: "This generation copies [books] onto papyrus and parchment and leaves them unused on the window ledge."

In the seventeen hundred years since the hermit complained about his contemporaries' reading habits, little, really, has changed, and little, I expect, will change. Every epoch has its doomsayers and its dusty papyrus that nobody reads. And every age has its bibliophiles as well as its scribblers who, oddly enough, take as a clarion call for papers the last verse of the Gospel according to John: "There are also many other things that Jesus did," writes John, adding, "if every one of them were written down, I suppose the world itself could not contain the books that would be written."

The world may never contain enough window ledges to hold or readers to read all the books, yet to be written, that some of us have in us. We write books anyway, because it is not only John's conclusion that has us by the heart, it is his gospel's prologue, too: "And the Word became flesh and lived among us, and we have seen his glory." The Word is embodied and glorious. The Word is a long way from dead.

– Day 16 –

In Sickness

[Amma Syncletica said], "If illness weighs us down, let us not be sorrowful as though, because of the illness and the prostration of our bodies, we could not sing, for all these things are for our good, for the purification of our desires."

The Forgotten Desert Mothers, 49

The cyst turned out to be a mass. The mass turned out to be cancer. The cancer turned out to be aggressive. The lumpectomy would be insufficient; a mastectomy was recommended. The mastectomy would be followed by a long and probably sickening course of chemotherapy. "It's just life," sighed the woman in whose body, in whose very breast, this cellular drama was unfolding. She was neither surprised nor terrified. Life went this way sometimes. She had nursed her own sick mother, and then her ailing husband. She knew illness and its ways of weighing us down. Because she had been acquainted with loved ones' infirmities, she was not made especially sorrowful by her own. Others' suffering had prepared her well for the damage her own disease might do. Her heart did not exactly *sing* as she underwent treatment for cancer, but neither did her heart go silent. It beat a drum as it always had done.

Was this steadfast woman any wiser than the guy who panicked and spun into a petulant depression upon learning of his own disturbing diagnosis? Years—if he was lucky—of strange and costly medications, administered invasively, lay before him, promising him a life he was now no longer certain he wanted to live. He'd survived a gunshot wound in battle, decades of cigarettes, and one case of soul-searing grief. He was tough, or so he'd thought until the doctor told him his condition was manageable but not curable. Manageable. That's what you called a pain-in-the-ass employee until you found a chance to fire him. Sure, you could fire your doctor, but you'd still be sick. It was the sick man's powerlessness that boggled him and laid him so low he felt like God's jilted girlfriend, eating cookies on the couch, watching daytime TV, feeling sorry as hell for himself. He hated his heart, his own heart, for thumping incessantly in the middle of the mess his life had become.

There's no right or wrong way to be sick, and no way not to be sick someday. Some people face illness resolutely, as Jesus set his face toward Jerusalem, and some people go to Gethsemane when they're sick, fighting mightily and prayerfully against the thing that threatens them. My own husband lies sick in bed as I write this. It's a minor enough ailment; he'll sleep it off. But one day, one of us will get something that sleep alone won't cure. Will we be circumspect and accepting, like the woman facing the surgical removal of her breast, or blindsided like the man with the incurable condition? The answer to this may depend on something other than psychological temperament—something spiritual, such as our understanding of illness and healing and God.

Amma Syncletica of Egypt was a Desert Mother who, having grown up in Alexandria, lived a stripped-down existence in a tomb outside the city, and there came to understand sickness as cleansing and redemptive. "These things," she said of "illness and the prostration of our bodies . . . are for our good, for the purification of our desires."

Syncletica is said to have died in her eighties, after suffering for three years from cancer. Long before she succumbed to this disease, didn't Syncletica's life of austerity, prayer, and service to the women she served as a spiritual guide purify her of ungodly desires? In the end did any traces of mean selfishness remain within her, requiring obliteration by cancer? Apparently she thought so. Spiritual purification is all Syncletica lived for, and nothing of life fell outside God's purview and purposes. Perhaps, as the cancer cells multiplied and mutated in her flesh, she interpreted her resultant weakness and pain as means by which her last desires were made compassionate and intercessory. Maybe illness ultimately taught Syncletica, as it can teach us today, to strengthen the fainthearted, support the weak, help the suffering, and honor all people.

Disease has power to gentle us. I have known too many kindly ailing people not to believe this. Sickness doesn't usually alter a personality completely, but it can sweeten and even dissolve the bitter and the sour parts of a soul. In hospital rooms, despite the constant invasions of privacy, the restless roommates and bland food (not to mention other vagaries of health care), patients often become just that—patient. Of course, some people would say submission to suffering is no virtue and visualize disease as an enemy within to be vanquished. But others refuse this contemplative reproduction of violence and undergo a subtler, more vulnerable healing process that doesn't posit self-will as a conqueror or god, but as, to borrow Amma Syncletica's perspective, a desire to be purified, made into a holier yearning than the brute will to live. In my experience, people who are sick often want to be of service. I think of a woman incrementally recovering from reconstructive surgery, knitting blanket after blanket to be wrapped around children in Intensive Care. I remember a boy who had undergone heart surgery at age three. Years later he looked after his grandmother and his goldfish with equal devotion.

"Do not go gentle," the poet Dylan Thomas urged his old and ailing father, whose robust health Thomas couldn't stand to see drain away. "Do Not Go Gentle Into That Good Night" is the poet's "greatest hit," perhaps because the poem's many admirers identify not only with Thomas's grief but also with his raging fear of human weaknesses and mortality. In a youth-obsessed society with forty-five million uninsured citizens, "Rage, rage against the dying of the light" is not surprisingly a more popular attitude toward illness than is Amma Syncletica's teaching that physical infirmities "are for our good." But Syncletica doesn't counsel masochism or mere passive surrender to sickness. She admonishes us not to indulge in any self-pitying fantasy that we deserve immunity to ill health. She's gutsy. She looks squarely at the human condition, accepts it entirely, and implores us to do the same, even to the daring point of giving thanks for the power of illness to purify our wants and make us finally capable of going gently into God's welcoming embrace.

– Day 17 –

Mind Your Mind

A brother asked Abba Joseph, saying, "What should I do, for I do not have the strength to bear evil, nor to work for charity's sake?" The old man said to him, "If you cannot do any of these things, at least guard your conscience from all evil with regard to your neighbor and you will be saved."

The Sayings of the Desert Fathers, 102–103

Yesterday I met a colleague for tea. She is new in town, a clergywoman and a writer, like me. We sat across from each other in an otherwise empty café in the late afternoon. Her tea was hot and green, mine blackberry flavored and iced. I asked her about her work, and she described some articles she had published on rich and fascinating topics for a readership of worship leaders. She spoke of sacramental things: "the table," "the font," "the Word." Then she asked me what I'm writing. For an instant I worried that my literary accomplishments wouldn't measure up to hers. Then I told her, "a collection of reflections on sayings of the Desert Fathers and Mothers." Her eyes brightened with interest, and I felt, well, interesting, not to mention smart and deep. Later I admitted to myself what I must internally acknowledge several times a week: *The Ego Has Landed.*

Reader, make no mistake. I write this book not because I have mastered the wisdom of the desert monastics, but because I have not. I write this book so that you and I might consider together the teachings of our elders, who know the folly of thinking ourselves interesting, smart, deep, in any way better—or for that matter, worse—than our neighbors.

"What should I do?" a young monk in the desert once asked an elder named Abba Joseph. "I do not have the strength to bear evil, nor to work for charity's sake."

I identify with this younger, worried monk. He knows he is far from attaining the fortitude and generosity of his teacher. He looks around his small and prayerful community in the Egyptian town of Panephysis and sees others performing extraordinary acts of courage and kindness the likes of which he has never attempted. I look around Tucson, Arizona and I see the pastor of a church near my home, working for charity's sake, organizing efforts to bring lifesaving supplies to impoverished migrants crossing the desert to find jobs, they hope. When, on a June day, in a blazing, uninhabited area, the pastor comes upon the decomposing body of a nineteen-year-old Mexican woman whose traveling companions had to leave her behind lest they die along with her, surely he must summon the strength to bear evil.

What should I do, what should any of us do? You may not live near a blistering border policed by National Guard troops, but you do live in this world, and someone not far from where you sit reading is suffering now, needlessly and unjustly. You may not possess the means or the strength to change that person's life, but you can, according to Abba Joseph, change your mind for the better, or protect it from changing into a force for mercilessness and unkindness. "At least guard your conscience from all evil with regard to your neighbor," counsels Abba Joseph.

It is not as easy as it sounds. Mentally resisting selfish allurements takes effort, practice, and even more of God's grace. My new colleague, the one who writes about Christian sacraments, might tell you: the bath that is baptism, the meal that is Eucharist, the Word that is Christ—these have much to do with the shaping and guarding of your mind, the cultivation within you of love for your neighbor. So go to church, regularly, for God's sake. Worship God with other people, and do it well. Like no other habit, this one will help you claim the salvation that Abba Joseph says a person with a cleansed and watchful conscience can know.

"You will be saved," Abba Joseph assured the anxious monk, and by extension assures you and me. I, for one, study the words of the *abbas* and the *ammas*, I write in response to them not to demonstrate my smarts or depth, but to know the saving grace of Christ as our elders knew it. This book is my searching answer to the question, "What should I do?"

Perhaps like you, I did not always know what to do with my life. Like the uncertain monk who sought Abba Joseph's guidance, I measured myself against others and found I did not measure up to them or their efforts to resist evil and work for the well-being of others. At my least confident I resented the good people I failed to emulate. The Christian activists I knew looked impossibly noble, with their volunteerism among the smelly homeless guys who slept in the shelter downstairs at the church. Compared with the death penalty abolitionist who possessed all the zeal—and charm—of a biblical prophet, I felt sheltered and irrelevant. I was awed by the local Catholic Worker who'd renounced all his army brat privilege to get by on ten dollars a week and agitate for social change. I was a writer. I spent hours making sentences and verses of poetry that might never accomplish a single apparently constructive purpose. I was none of the righteous people I begrudgingly admired. I couldn't manage even a lousy imitation of them.

Nor would Abba Joseph recommend I try. This wise desert elder did not advise the uncertain monk to imitate those Christians combating evil and working for charity to whom the young man unhappily compared himself. Abba Joseph took the monk as he came, and respected his self-assessment. In urging him to guard his conscience with regard to his neighbors, Joseph seemed to sense, and offer an antidote to, the monk's temptation to castigate himself or the local do-gooders and their beneficiaries.

Know yourself; be true to yourself; watch yourself; correct yourself. This is the essence of Joseph's advice, and it is as good today as it ever was. If we put it into practice, by God's grace you and I may find we are unlikely to indulge in delusion, pretense, carelessness, and arrogance. A community peopled with souls guided by Joseph's counsel to guard one's own conscience would be a neighborly place inhabited by reflective, authentic, and humble men and women. This sounds a lot like a blessed world, a world with room enough in it for everyone, including activists and writers, monks and seekers, you and me.

– Day 18 –

The Cross of Solitude

Born around 334 C.E., Asella and her sister Marsella were members of a noble and wealthy Roman family. . . . Asella consecrated herself to God when she was ten years of age. . . . Jerome describes her life in a narrow cell in her family's home in Rome: "Enclosed in the confines of a single cell, she enjoyed the wide pastures of paradise. The same patch of earth existed as her place both of prayer and of rest. Fasting was her recreation and hunger her refreshment. If she took food, it was not from love of eating but from human exhaustion, and the bread, salt, and cold water to which she restricted herself sharpened more than appeased her appetite." . . . Jerome mentions her sale of a gold necklace . . . . The money was given to the poor.

The Forgotten Desert Mothers, 73–74

Lightning in the night sky—brief, bright veins
in the back of God's black hand—
make a momentary day of the darkness I pray into at
    my window.
Mortared marble frames my narrow view of the earth,
but it's heaven where I live,
having died to the wealth I once enjoyed.

Oh, Rome, you rotting jewel box of an empire.
I hardly expect you to comprehend my calling,
the long death I've chosen to undergo for Christ.
Even my sister wishes I would wear
white silks once in a while, or smile, or chat
the way we used to. But even as a child,
I knew I was meant to be the Lord's widow.
I was destined for great love and loss,
the cross of solitude.

Jerome approves. He and Palladius
pay me periodic visits. Their talk, infused
with names of holy things unseen by most Romans,
illumines like lightning my dark anchorhold,
this tomb of my dead self.
Before I died to the world, to feed the poor,
I sold a gold necklace, the precious, strangling heirloom
my father had intended for my dowry.
Unceremoniously, as I wished, I was buried,
then reconceived, alone and anew in this cool womb,
my convent for one where darkness is as light,
and I am no one's daughter but the Father's,
no one's sister but the Son's.

– Day 19 –
The Outcast of All

[Abba Nilus] said, "Happy is the monk who thinks he is the outcast of all."

The Sayings of the Desert Fathers, 154

There once was a goat, an unremarkable creature with spindly but strong gray legs and a little mouth curved into a faint and enigmatic smile. The goat had two hard horns and two pointed ears, and these stuck out from the top of its head like a crown. Nevertheless, the goat was unremarkable, except perhaps for its tendency to look people straight in the eye. The goat's eyes were dull gold with black slits for irises. The goat lived only to mow the grass, but people found its frank gaze incriminating. "Lose the goat," the people said. "Get that goat out of here." Finally the people struck upon a slogan: "The goat must go." They felt powerful and unified as they repeated it, although they couldn't say why or explain their deepening, shared aversion to the goat. Someone poked the goat in the side with a stick. It bleated and resumed chewing. But the poking continued, rhythmically, getting more aggressive all the time, and the people began to chant, "The goat must go, the goat must go," until the harmless, bewildered beast left town. The relieved, delighted people changed their slogan to "The goat is gone! The goat is gone!" But soon they grew tired of saying even this, and started looking for another goat to pick on.

"Happy are you when you think you are the outcast of all."

And what would be the punch line of this beatitude, had Abba Nilus supplied it? Maybe: "For you shall be welcomed." Only a true welcome—warm, unconditional acceptance by others—can heal, over time, an outcast's wounds and bring happiness so sweet it's unmistakably of God. Abba Nilus's beatitude works as Jesus' beatitudes work: according to a promised blessing only God can give. When relief and comfort finally come, the alternative to agony is so intense it's paradise.

Psychologists and wise spiritual teachers and scapegoats know: to be an outcast is agony. Notice that Abba Nilus's outcast only *thinks* he is the outcast of all. There may in fact be a silent majority who have neither cast him out nor made a point to receive him. No matter. If even a few members of your community actively revile you, you're as good as exiled, and soon you'll be as gone as that old goat.

Good church people, fine Christians, sometimes behave very badly for the sake of congregational cohesion. And a wounded person leads them.

There once was a woman whose father had violated her sexually when she was a child. That was decades earlier, but the unspeakable trauma of incest had infected her psyche like a virus that would flare up in her conduct, which was by turns kittenish and wolfish. When she wasn't flattering you and bringing you gifts she was obsessing on your mistakes and how to rid the church of you, because you, you were the problem, the threat, and before you had arrived on the scene all had been lovely and harmonious, but now things were changing, and too fast, and this is not what we wanted, not at all what we had in mind. This isn't how we do things around here. Let me tell you how we do things around here. We circle the wagons. We discuss the problem, and the problem is you. I'm sorry: the problem *is* you. But God will resolve it. God will restore us. God is with us, right now. Right now, God is with us. Let us pray.

The scapegoating rituals that communities under stress resort to are anti-baptismal. Whereas baptism is the sacrament of cleansing and inclusion, scapegoating rituals are dirtying and exclusionary, a fundamentally unholy means by which a community recovers its unity and equilibrium.

There once was a Muslim, Pakistani psychologist and consultant to the United Nations who addressed an auditorium full of Christians. "Humans need a dark side," he said. "An object of the projection of evil. If you treat people as evil, they become that. When Western authorities interrogate me aggressively at customs, I begin to wonder if I am somehow evil, somehow a terrorist."

"Happy are you when you think you are the outcast of all."
Happy are you when the power-clique brunches without you, forking their succulent omelets as though they were your dead body, calling you selfish, a used-car salesman, laughing deliciously, agreeing they could never confide in you, never trust you. You simply have the wrong kind of soul. "It's sad," they say, grinning. "We're bad. God knows we're bad. Here's to us!" And they raise their coffee cups: "To us!"
Happy are you in your strange new city, befriending a guy whose wife just left him, again. He loves your company. You are kind. But you have your limits. Of his misery there is only so much you can take. You glance at your watch, again, and extend your hand as though you two have come to some agreement. You insist on paying for the drinks "because that's what friends do," and go home to have a long soak. The bathroom is as good a cell as any.
Happy are you when your face, fish-eye-reflected in the bathtub faucet, is all nose, and your chin and mouth recede,

and your small eyes, blinking and bloodshot, recede. But they drip—your eyes—copiously, and rings form and expand on the bathwater's surface, and then the rings disappear.

It can't end here.

Actually, it could end here.

Some of it should end here: the victimizing, the perpetual victimizing. The devastating doing unto others must end. Fantasize all you will about revenge, but in the end, pray your confession and leave nothing out. Say your amen and climb out of the tub. The water's gone cold, so pull the plug and watch it drain away. Dry off. Day is done. Now lay you down to sleep. The goat is gone. Happy are you. Let us pray.

– Day 20 –
Good Vigilantes

We sail on in darkness. The psalmist calls our life a sea and the sea is either full of rocks, or very rough, or else it is calm. We are like those who sail on a calm sea, and seculars are like those on a rough sea. We always set our course by the sun of justice, but it can often happen that the secular is saved in tempest and darkness, for he keeps watch as he ought, while we go to the bottom through negligence, although we are on a calm sea . . .

The Forgotten Desert Mothers, 62

In a small glass frame on my desk I keep a postcard I bought for three dollars on eBay. According to the message, fountain penned on October 18, 1948 by Mrs. H. Boinski, the weather in Tucson, Arizona, where she had arrived three days earlier, was fine. The postcard's recipient, Mrs. I. Kozakiewicz, lived in Chicago, where the weather was probably pretty mild as well. "Did your people find anything out? How are you? Drop me a card some time," wrote Mrs. Boinski to Mrs. Kozakiewicz.

Sixty years later, some of Mrs. Kozakiewicz's people probably still reside in Chicago. I spent thirty-four years in that city, and I know the neighborhood where Mrs. Kozakiewicz lived. I can imagine her graystone three-flat on Logan Boulevard. Like many Chicagoans, she was perhaps a faithful Roman Catholic.

She may have attended the parish church about a block west of her home. And surely she was intrigued by the picture on Mrs. Boinski's postcard—a gaudy watercolor illustration of Tucson's Benedictine Sanctuary of Perpetual Adoration. The Spanish Colonial–style monastery stands, pink, gold, and grand against the backdrop of the Rincon Mountain Range.

For most of the years since I moved to Tucson I have been an oblate—a non-monastic affiliate—of the Benedictine Sisters of Perpetual Adoration. I live two miles from their monastery on Country Club Road. You might think I would pray there daily, and indeed, during some seasons I have done so. But this year I have spent much of my time newly solo-pastoring a Presbyterian congregation while also writing this book. At 7:30 in the morning, when the sisters are beginning the liturgy of Lauds by standing to genuflect and sing, "O God, come to my assistance; O Lord, make haste to help me," I am usually sitting down at my laptop computer with a cup of coffee and a silent prayer that, like the supplication of my monastic friends, says more or less *God help me.* I glance at my framed postcard of the monastery I love, then write for a while about monastic watchfulness before saving my document and driving to work.

Sometimes I cheat. Sometimes I check my e-mail before focusing on my manuscript. I want to see if my Mrs. Kozakiewicz has "dropped me a card," telling me how she and her people are doing. My Mrs. Kozakiewicz is really a clergywoman and dear friend who lives in Illinois. You might say she talked me into my present ministry by preaching at my service of installation. But more than this, my friend is a vigilante, not in the outlaw sense of that term (although she might like that idea), but in the sense that she keeps vigil. She is alert, watchful, responsive, attuned to the hazards and holiness inherent in these Christian lives we lead. The virtue of vigilance is written all over her blog. Unlike the countless dull and narcissistic sneeze diaries cluttering the World Wide Web, my friend's blog is a witty record of a life lived observantly. Take, for example, this item from a little litany of "Sunday Thoughts" she posted recently: "A woman at church complimented me this morning and said I was 'finally wearing enough makeup.' Do male pastors get harassed about their appearance so much? Sheesh."

I tell myself it's hardly cheating at all; in fact, it's necessary for me to check my e-mail for messages from my Mrs. Kozakiewicz. For I am, after a fashion, Mrs. Boinski, and I live in a desert, a dry and thirsty place—yes, just two miles from the Benedictine Sanctuary of Perpetual Adoration, but it's been a while since I prayed there and had my adoration tuned up, my perpetuity checked. Like the fourth-century Christian pilgrims who trekked into the desert to seek spiritual guidance from wise monastic teachers, I need a word. I need Mrs. Kozakiewicz to drop me a card. I need my vigilante friend to tell me what she notices today. What she notices today is that people often notice superfluous things when they could be hearing the Gospel.

"I have a question for you preachers out there," my friend tells the readers of her blog." Which response would you rather receive when shaking hands in the narthex after a sermon? (A) You know, I *never* thought about it like that. (B) You know, that is *so* true."

Both responses imply parishioners' alertness to the Gospel preached rather than, say, excessive interest in the preacher's mascara. Clearly, my friend has faith in her flock's capacity to notice the message and not merely the medium. But she knows what her people are up against, how hard it can be for everyday Christians to keep watch for God breaking into the world when it's so much easier to spend our awareness on other concerns, frivolous or substantive: cosmetic makeovers, presidential campaigns.

Those who occasionally visit monasteries, the Mrs. Boinskis of the world, sometimes imagine that life within the cloister is blessedly free of the superficial allurements that compete for the attention all Christians are called to pay to God. No monastic, we are tempted to think, would ever miss the point of the day's scripture reading because someone's appearance was too distracting. But what about the time I was on retreat at a monastery and sat in on the intimate midday prayers of the residents? One of them openly giggled at my efforts to maintain modesty despite my wraparound skirt, which kept flapping open. Later that day, beneath the open second-story window of the guest apartment where I was lodging, the same vowed monastic cried out, "Juliet! Juliet!"

Wardrobe malfunctions and individual craziness within religious communities are not the only distractions faced by cloistered contemplatives, who don't necessarily find it any easier to practice prayerful vigilance than do their secular counterparts. Indeed, to keep alert within the placid stability of the monastery can be harder than staying awake amid a noisy, multitasking society. So says Amma Syncletica of Egypt. She was a Desert Christian who enjoyed social privilege during her youth in fourth-century Alexandria but later renounced her wealth to live a life of prayer in an unused tomb outside the city. Apparently drawn to Syncletica by her profound spiritual vigilance, a number of women formed a monastery where they could learn from her the arts of attentiveness. Syncletica allowed her disciples to harbor no illusions about the simplicity of monastic life. While she likened monastics to "those who sail on a calm sea," and seculars to "those on a rough sea," Syncletica affirmed this rough sea as a saving grace that makes good vigilantes of secular Christians, who must keep watch for God amid "tempest and darkness"—complex, unpredictable lives.

The darker and choppier the waters, the more rattled and unenlightened we are, the sharper our wakefulness. To the panicking boatmen who found Jesus asleep on a cushion in the stern as a gale threatened to capsize their craft, this would have been good news. To the rest of us, who rarely seem to sail on a calm sea or find time to retreat in a monastery, it is good news, too, that even our high anxieties play a necessary part in the drama of our salvation. Faced with tempest and darkness, most of us do our best to batten down the hatches and make the best of things. We take care of our people and even manage, sometimes, to stay in touch with faraway friends. Sure, we suffer the occasional bout of insomnia, but sleeplessness can be converted to good vigilance, by faith. Restless we may be, but we're keeping watch as we ought to. Thus, by God (and according to Amma Syncletica), are we saved.

– Day 21 –
In My Cell

A brother came to Scetis to visit Abba Moses and asked him for a word. The old man said to him, "Go, sit in your cell, and your cell will teach you everything."

The Sayings of the Desert Fathers, 139

Paris Hilton told Larry King she didn't care for the bologna sandwiches they fed her in jail. I admit: those jail sandwiches are awfully dry, and the bologna slices—absurdly thin, mere flavoring. Still, your cell will teach you everything if you sit in it long enough. When she was locked up, Paris Hilton sensed this to be true, as her exclusive, post-release interview with *People* magazine revealed. She spoke of "the nun who works at the jail for all the ladies. She would come every day and we would pray."[6]

Perhaps, back in 1984, if I had stayed for longer than three hours in my cell at the jail on Chicago's west side, a nun would have come and prayed with me, too. I didn't know how to pray on my own; I didn't believe there was a God to pray to. I sometimes think that if someone had been there early in my life to teach me about Jesus, and if there had been a Sunday School where I could have learned a few sweet songs and decent values, and later, a youth group where the other kids and I could have talked about Important Issues and developed crushes on each other, then maybe shoplifting would not have been quite so compelling to me, or recreational drugs and reckless relationships, for that matter.

Never having been to Sunday School, I cannot personally attest to its positive influence on children and their later development. But I know some upstanding adults who had lots of Sunday Schooling as kids and no criminal activity as young adults, and thus I see a correlation between the two; I surmise that church can be good for children, help keep them off the streets and out of the slammer. In the women's unit at California and Western the cells lined one side of the corridor, and we occupants could not see each other's faces. But the others could hear the telltale clanking when I was being locked in.

"Oooh, girl. What'd you do to get yourself in here?" one woman called to me from another cell.

"You don't want to know," I answered, stalling.

Several women shouted, "Oh, yes we do!"

I was glad they couldn't see my face, young and puffy from crying, or my fried, frizzy hair. "I stole a ninety-eight cent package of hair conditioner from Sally Beauty Supply."

"You did *what?*"

"Don't make me repeat it."

"You're in here for ninety-eight *cent?* Guard, let this poor bitch go!"

I had made roughly the same plea to the two patrolmen in the squad car, who had spared me the humiliation of handcuffs but had refused to drop me off at my apartment on the drive to the police station.

"Why did you steal the item?" one of the officers had asked me as I rode in the backseat, miserably watching through the squad car's grimy windows as city dwellers at liberty walked their dogs and ran their errands.

"Because I ruined my hair with a home perm and I needed deep conditioner. The stupid thing is, I didn't have to steal it. I had the money."

"That's the stupid thing, all right."

This was the extent of my conversation with the cops. At the station they turned me over to a policewoman who asked me to follow her into a drab room where, before frisking me, she said, "You got any needles in your pockets? I don't want to get stuck."

"I stole hair conditioner," I told her morosely. "I'm not a junkie."

"I gotta ask," she said, patting me down.

Indeed, she had to ask. In the jail, once the other detainees had finally gotten over their loud disbelief at the pettiness of my theft, a woman whose voice came from the cell next to mine said dreamily, "My pimp's gonna get me out and get my fix and everything's gonna be fine."

What do you say to that: *How nice for you*? I was a dropout English major with ruined hair. I'd misbehaved, but I didn't know from pimps and heroin. So I kept my mouth shut, except, after a while, to eat the scrawny bologna sandwich an armed guard delivered through the cell bars.

And then I made myself as comfortable as possible on my stainless steel plank. Before drifting off to sleep I let myself feel the institutional loneliness of my cell, and half-listened to other detainees' conversations about children, jewelry, and the last time they were here. They inhabited the jail with a familiarity and ease that reminded me of other women I had encountered, wearing hospital gowns and elaborate manicures, chatting casually in the waiting room of an abortion clinic.

I had long felt cocooned and immune in my life, a good girl gone bad, but mildly, without much in the way of repercussions. This is apparently how Paris Hilton felt about her high-profile life, until that California judge sent her back to jail a second time, "to face," as Hilton (or her handlers) put it, "the consequences of violating probation." The sayings of the Desert Fathers and Mothers weren't, to my knowledge, among the stacks of spiritual materials Hilton read during her incarceration, but her later words to Larry King—"Don't serve the time; let the time serve you"[7]—are surprisingly reminiscent of Abba Moses' classic insight: "Go, sit in your cell, and your cell will teach you everything."

If a decadent heiress and socialite is capable of facing herself, her demons, and her God in a jail cell—and Paris Hilton is capable of this—then I am, too, and we all are. This is not to say I found Jesus in jail. (I would not find Jesus for another three years, in the apartment I shared with my Presbyterian boyfriend.) But my jail cell made me feel my sad and itchy need for salvation, though at the time I would not have described the feeling in these terms. With its empty walls, metal toilet, and friendly, disembodied din of busted prostitutes' remarks, with its lack of any personal contents but I, who felt like not much of a person, my jail cell prompted me to wonder why I kept getting into trouble—dropping out of college and shoplifting and nightclubbing for fun and having in fact no fun, but rather coming home late and alone to a studio apartment, cramped and cellular in its own right, full of nothing but a dopey girl for whom posting bail hardly seemed a worthy investment.

Your jail cell, your studio apartment, your bathroom, your room at the retreat center, the racket in your head, the fertile silence that comes after the racket finally dies down, these will teach you everything God already knows about you. God is your cell mate, and with God you have no secrets, no criminal record, no shame, nothing but truthfulness and redemption by love. Your cell will teach you everything. Just ask Abba Moses. Ask Paris Hilton. Or ask this pastor. I'll gladly teach you everything my cell taught me.

– Day 22 –

Don't Lose Yourself

Macarius said, "Do not lose yourself in order to save another."

The Desert Fathers, 24

Dear friend, I am no mother. I love my nieces and nephews, but I don't know what it is to love a child with the fierce attachment of a good parent. When you were my age, you didn't know, either. "I don't do children," is what you said. But then you fell in love with someone who did children compulsively. It's ugly to say it like that, but I know what I saw in her: a driving need to rescue as many foster kids as the system would let her take in. She looked like a hero, a saint, a real-life Mother Hubbard. She had a way with crack babies.

One baby in particular had spent the first months of her life strapped in a car seat in a drug house, subsisting on peanut butter and cow's milk, when someone thought to feed her. The back of her malleable skull had been malformed by the constant pressure of the molded plastic seat, and her eyes looked faraway when they should have achieved the direct, mystic gaze of a child beholding her mother. But her mother was gone, down the killing black hole of addiction, and soon after the Amber Alert was sounded, the child was found, malnourished but alive. The child entered The System and The System placed the child with the woman you loved.

A decade earlier, another foster child had died in this woman's care. She told me the story: a fever overtook the little girl. The heat in her infected body rose to the breaking point, but never broke. The fever held steady and hot, but *the idiot at pediatric ER called me an overprotective parent and sent us home.* The fever climbed higher and higher until it carried the child away on a merciless wave of red mercury. *By the time we made it back to the hospital, she was dead.* In the waiting room, the woman blacked out from shock. Someone drove her home, and soon, uniformed police appeared at the door, asking questions. Wild with sorrow, she flew at them. Someone had to hold her back, hold her down. It was you.

You loved her, trauma and all, and this was not her first trauma. She had a history, familial and hideous and too deep to heal. Some wounds stay wounds, and such was your beloved's heart: a clenching fist, bloodied by its gloves-off brawl with life. For her, conflict was to love as iron is to blood: enriching. She knew how to rescue desperate babies, but hadn't a clue how to love an adult.

Believe it or not, you are learning to live without her, and grief is your teacher. Grief, feral and outraged, is not killing you, although you feel it is, and sometimes you wish it would. Love that was not love was your crucifixion, and grief, which is love that is stronger than death, is raising you up from the dead. I'll be your Thomas. I'll thrust my hand in your side and say *my Lord and God*, if that's what it takes to help you claim your new, naked life. You are raw to the world, and the future will not be some banal repetition of what you already know, and know to be false. Your life has been stripped of such scant consolations as a night without derision or your hand held for just five minutes *if it will please shut you up.*

Your life, too, has been robbed—no, let me put it properly: she has robbed you of the children you grew to love in spite of yourself. You worked at a job I never once heard you say you enjoyed, to clothe and feed the children and dig their backyard swimming pool and take them to vacation theme parks. You were the breadwinner and the loser of your self-respect as their foster mother crowded in more and more kids and used them to shield herself from her pain and your needs, which were simply human, not the outrageous demands she told you they were. You needed her to love you. You needed her to save you some shred of herself. But there was always a child and another child for her to take in, and in the end she denied you even a playdate with them, unless you did as she told you and let her exploit and insult you. The kids, whom the overburdened foster care system underserved, became bargaining chips in her custody: you do her bidding and you see them, or you don't, and you don't.

You don't see the children these days. You're waiting, weighing your options, wondering what a lawyer might do, given a $5,000 retainer. You don't see the children these days because you don't see their mother, and you don't see yourself as a martyr.

"Don't lose yourself in order to save another," a man named Macarius said long ago. Martyrdom only increases the body count. To lose yourself would be a great loss to the rest of us, who love you in our human but wholehearted ways. None of us is anyone else's savior. Like me, like the children, like their foster mother and their lost birth parents, like The System, like you, all of us need saving. And we are being saved, made alive by a love that's been stabbed in the side but stands purified. We're all being saved by love with the palms of its hands gashed-through but no longer bleeding. *My Lord*, love was dead. *My God*, love is resurrected. The old love that was never love is over and gone and salvation is come. Love is Christ crucified—risen, this day. Salvation is you, saying, *I am not powerless*. Salvation is Christ making it true.

– Day 23 –
Love and Anger

Sisois once said with confidence, "For thirty years I have not prayed to God without sin. When I pray, I say 'Lord Jesus Christ, protect me from my tongue.' Even now, it causes me to fall every day."

The Desert Fathers, 26

This morning I climbed out of bed at six thirty and deleted about one-third of the sermon titled "Love and Anger" that I would be preaching later in the morning. It's not that the section I deleted was angry. On the contrary, it was conflict-avoidant. It stalled and meandered, and I woke up knowing it, so out it went.

In church, I climbed into the pulpit and read, from the Gospel of Luke, one of the most unpleasant passages in the New Testament. My voice almost left me as I spoke these words of Jesus:

> I came to bring fire to the earth, and how I wish it were already kindled! I have a baptism with which to be baptized, and what stress I am under until it is completed! Do you think that I have come to bring peace to the earth? No, I tell you, but rather division! From now on five in one household will be divided, three against two and two

> against three; they will be divided: father against son and
> son against father, mother against daughter and daughter
> against mother, mother-in-law against her daughter-in-law
> and daughter-in-law against mother-in-law. (12:49-53)

And then I preached the sermon, which came straight to the point. We are called to maintain loving self-control, to be angry, but not sin. Of course, we fail to fulfill this calling. We get angry, and we anger God. So we need the forgiveness and mercy of God, which are even more abundant than our anger and sin. "This past week's spectacular examples of humankind's propensity to be angry *and* sin," I said to the congregation, "include the shooting of worshipers in a Missouri church and a massive suicide bombing in Iraq that killed 175 people." I went on, "The trouble with examples like these of the monstrous ways human beings act that infuriate God—other than the obvious horror and tragedy of the events—is the way ordinary Christians like you and I can dismiss these examples: *I'm not a homicidal maniac*, we might say. *It's not me God's angry at. I'm a perfectly nice person. I'm not aggressive. I'm not a sinner.* But let's get real. Who among us has not felt momentary or even more than momentary rage toward someone we cherish who has disappointed us beyond words? Who has never acted on such a feeling? Who hasn't spoken hurtfully, in anger? I'm not asking for a show of hands here, but if we did deny it, I do suspect Jesus would have two very hard words to say to us: *You hypocrites*."

After the service, as I greeted worshipers, a woman on her way out of the church told me, "You're speaking right to my family."

A man shook my hand, smiled, and said, "Were you preaching to me?" I laughed and told him, "I was preaching for all of us. I was preaching for myself."

Later, I listened privately to one parishioner in particular, struggling with great pain and anger. And then I listened to that person's hurting spouse.

I came home and talked with a friend with whom I have a relationship that I liken to a pastry—layered, rich, complex, and sweet, with hints of unexpected tartness, which I expressed today in the form of a snobbish, disapproving remark. She responded, "I love you too, you creep."

And what stress I am under. Dare I identify with those words of the infuriated Jesus and claim stress as my excuse?

Or shall I delete the extraneous material, come straight to the point, and with a desert monk named Sisois, pray, *Lord Jesus Christ, protect me from my tongue (and protect other people, while you're at it. Protect them from their tongues. Protect them from mine.)*?

Often I find that parishioners are surprised by my sermons' relevance to their lives, including their daily stresses and interpersonal conflicts. Sometimes people tell me I'm unusually perceptive about their struggles. But I doubt I am. Mostly, I notice their humanity, my own, God's goodness, and the ways the Scriptures speak of all these.

"Where do you get your ideas for sermons?" a parishioner recently asked me after church.

"From the Scriptures," I told him.

"Oh, come on," he objected.

"No, really," I told him. "The Bible. I look for what the Bible is saying to our lives."

A lot of folks seem to expect the Bible to talk about something else, something other than human experience, something unfathomable they need a religious expert to explain.

And then it turns out, the Bible is largely about how pissed off and stressed out we all are.

I myself was surprised when I finally noticed this. Early on in my Christian life, even before I was baptized, I purchased a red-letter King James Version with a leatherette cover and took it on a camping trip with my boyfriend, to read in the car.

Forget it. I was no readier for the beautiful, antiquated diction of the KJV than I was to realize that faithfulness is an everyday mixture of decidedly unmystical human discipline and God's bottomless grace. For several years, I labored under the delusion that Christianity was esoteric and didn't deal in ugly stuff like anger. I kept looking for the grail, the insight, the answer that would bring me peace and make a really good Christian of me. This futile and misguided search of mine was the means God used to work on me when I wasn't looking, to help me learn what I know so far, which may not be much, but gets me from Sunday to Sunday. What I know so far includes this: We're mad. We're inclined to hurt one another. We must try not to. God helps us with our efforts at self-control. When we fail and we acknowledge it, God forgives us, in love.

These insights, by the way, are not original to me. I got them from the Bible. I read other books too—lately, books of sayings by long-ago Christians who, despite the fact that they did bizarre things like live alone in caves, were not unlike you and me. They were mad too. They too needed Jesus to keep them from giving voice to the vicious words in their heads and to forgive them when they failed to hold their tongues.

"Sometimes he beats me—with a comment," is a remark I once heard someone make about a beloved relation. I was shocked—more by the candor than the content of the comment. Most of us, most of the time, can't admit we're beaten without showing a bruise, or that we beat one another without lifting a finger. The tongue, that nasty, tasty muscle, articulates our rage. It causes us and causes others to fall, every day.

But the tongue also prays: *Lord Jesus, protect me.* And for every human tongue, there is a God, with ears. God hears. And God hauls us back up. Every day.

– Day 24 –

In the Desert, They Are Burned

Poemen said, "It is written, 'Like as the hart longs for the waterbrooks, so longs my soul for you, O my God' (Ps 42:1). Indeed, the harts in the desert eat many snakes and when their venom makes them burn with thirst they come to the waters to assuage their burning thirst. It is the same for monks: in the desert they are burned by the poison of the demons and they long for Saturday and Sunday to come so that they can go to the springs of water, that is, the Body and Blood of the Lord, to be purified from the poison of the evil ones."

The Desert Fathers, 192

In the summer the whole Sonoran Desert longs for water. The soil, dry and browned as toast, hardens under the sun, and vegetation turns the same colorless color as the soil. The heat, a brooding presence, tackles you as you set foot outside.

One summer afternoon I stepped out of my church office into the blazing midday, then hurried back into the sealed indoors. I e-mailed my husband: "It's so hot out I think I can smell soil burning." He replied: "That's the smell of all hell breaking loose."

I suddenly felt so fatigued I had to lie down right then, on the couch in my office, where I succumbed to a fitful nap until I woke up in a sweat. The thermostat read 92 degrees—a dozen degrees lower than the temperature outside. That's when I realized the church's air conditioner had broken. The repairman came to church the next day and discovered that a pack rat had gotten caught in the air conditioner's motor and died. A few of us at church joked about how we really ought to quit practicing animal sacrifice.

A few days later, the skies went moody above us—sunlit to the east, dark and lightning-forked to the west, where the bulging clouds broke as they eventually do every summer. Rain fell hard on the desert for three consecutive days, calling up the astringent scent of creosote foliage, evoking from lifeless sticks succulent greenery. The weather service stated the obvious, declaring that the annual monsoon had arrived. The weather service also publicly wondered if they should rename the Sonoran monsoon "the summer storm season," suggesting the latter term more clearly conveyed the danger of the wet, electrifying change in the weather.

No renaming was needed. To residents of Southern Arizona, monsoon means a verdant midsummer resurrection, but it also means driving wind and heavy rainfall. It means *get out of the swimming pool before you're electrocuted.* Monsoon means flooded arroyos and downed power lines. The electric company warns us with billboards in which a fallen, sparking cable morphs into an open-jawed sidewinder, poised to strike, lightning bolting from its fangs. A "summer storm" sounds vigorous, but not especially threatening, whereas the monsoon is a wild sky animal to whom we all pay due obeisance, scanning the clouds for ominous flashes, avoiding roads that the rains have turned into rivers.

Or most of us avoid such roads. Every year, despite bright yellow signs prohibiting entry into flooded washes, someone drives a car into deep water and has to be rescued, or hikes into a canyon on an overcast afternoon, to be thunderstruck by the monsoon's power. Renaming the monsoon seems unlikely to accomplish what is really required, which is a healthy measure of humility—our acknowledgment that we are small and fragile creatures up against a terrain and a climate that could swiftly do us in. Let's face it: a pack rat can take out our cooling and bring us to our knees. Think what six inches of rainfall can do.

Abba Poemen understood better than do many moderns that human beings are no match for the desert and its beasts: *the harts in the desert eat many snakes; in the desert they are burned by the poison of the demons.* Educated, present-day believers tend to get squeamish around such serpentine imagery, not for dread of the destructive powers snakes and demons represent, but for fear of literalism's current stranglehold on the religious imagination of many.

And then there is the Sonoran Desert. Here it is possible to consider scary, mythic creatures with an attitude something like what Marcus Borg has called "post-critical naïveté." In the desert, because we live quite literally among vipers, at one and the same time we can pride ourselves on being "post-critically" smart enough to know that snakes are not embodiments of Satan while we must also beware of those snakes that really could do us great harm.

At my church we have narrowly escaped such harm. During his regular rounds of the church property the exterminator came upon the skin of a diamondback rattlesnake in a bush near the Sunday School room. The church's Office Manager and I dropped what we were doing to hurry outside and behold the specimen. Curved along the corner of the multipurpose building, in the shade of a blooming Texas Ranger, the snakeskin lay, tubular, translucent, and patterned, with small, circular bulges where the snake's eyes had been. At the opposite end of the yard-long, remarkably intact molt was the tapering shape that once had held the rattle.

"Let's let it return to the earth," I suggested, backing away. Neither the exterminator nor the Office Manager disagreed.

The snakeskin, and the thought of the snake that had shed it, were awesome and untouchable, not unlike the snakes that those "harts" in Abba Poemen's desert clearly had no business eating. Of course snake venom made them burn with thirst. What else did they expect?

What do we expect when we build churches and homes in the habitats of desert-hearty rodents and reptiles? That animals will steer clear of our air conditioners and Sunday School rooms? We wish they would, but sometimes they don't, and so we've all got stories of our brushes with the desert's beasts: the bobcat in the moonlit parking lot, the hawk we saw disemboweling a dove in midair, the sickly little black bat that crept into the office and died.

For desert dwellers such images are somewhat commonplace yet still amazing, potent reminders of our vulnerable coexistence with the land's indigenous animal inhabitants. I remember the article I read in the Tucson newspaper about a local playwright who walked barefoot into his backyard one night. He startled a baby rattlesnake that had not yet developed the ability to control the amount of venom it injected into its victim. Having been born, as all rattlesnakes are, with a full supply of venom, the young snake apparently sank it all into the playwright's foot. After his hospitalization, the man spent weeks in a wheelchair.

"How would you describe the pain?" the newspaper journalist wanted to know.

The playwright answered, "unearthly," which seems as good a word as "demonic."

Perhaps, in his bitten, hobbled state the man came to dread the desert demons Abba Poemen spoke of centuries earlier. And perhaps, as he gradually regained the use of his foot, he came to reverence, as few of us will ever have to, the power of antivenom to exorcise and purify.

– Day 25 –
The Rest of Your Lives

Agatho said, "I tried never to go to sleep while I kept a grievance against anyone. Nor did I let anyone go to sleep while he had a grievance against me."

The Desert Fathers, 177

Rumor has it my brother got married a few weeks ago. He and his bride found an island locale that suited them, hired an officiant, and presumably invited a couple of friends to bear witness. I hear this much from my mother, who also tells me that my brother tells her that he tried to call me to tell me his good news but didn't want to leave me a voice message. Mildly miffed and disbelieving, I button back through the caller I.D., and what do you know, there's an unusual area code. I Google it to find it comes from my brother's neck of the world. Blest be the ties that bind.

I talk to my sister, who has talked to my brother. He sounds happy, she tells me.

We live all over the map, my family. We'll converge in Chicago at Thanksgiving, by which time, I pray, my brother and his bride will be happy still.

Can I blame them for keeping it on the down-low? What matters more than weddings is love, lasting and elastic.

My sister may remarry one day. I've made it clear: I'll be there, but I won't officiate. I just want to celebrate, be the maid of honor if she asks me to, not the *Mandy-there's-a-minister-handy.* I've done too many nod-to-God weddings as it is, having served as de facto chaplain for several of my husband's graduate students and other assorted couples, roughly half of whom are now divorced or contemplating it.

I recently bumped into the last couple at whose wedding I officiated. Fresh from their honeymoon, they looked radiant, holding hands on their way to the convenience store.

"Hi, Newlyweds," I said, and the bride gushed, "We're going to buy a lottery ticket! Think what we could do with thirty million dollars!"

"Just think!" I said. "Good luck!"

Later I sent her an e-mail: "So, did you win?"

"No," she replied, "but today I found out I'm pregnant, so it's the same, but with reverse cash flow."

Do people still get pregnant on their honeymoons? The idea seems quaint. Maybe this couple will do something else old-fashioned: stay married.

My husband Ken and I have been married for pushing twenty years. We marvel not only at our deepening love, but also at our good fortune, our relative rarity, what is becoming our longevity. But we've got nothing on some folks. During the Sunday morning sharing of joys and concerns my congregation bursts into applause whenever a couple announces some astonishing anniversary: fifty-three years, sixty years. They know well, it seems, Abba Agatho's wisdom: never go to sleep with a grievance against one another. Surely the decades have taught these old married couples other good habits that many young divorcees never found a way, or took the time, to learn.

A thrice-married friend in her seventies says of her second marriage, "It was a good affair. We should have left it at that."

Might I incorporate her quip into my premarital counseling with couples? It would make a provocative talking point. "Are you quite sure," I could ask them, "it isn't just a good affair you're after? Why marriage? If we deleted the wedding from the equation—canceled the florist, called off the caterer, fired the minister, and had the J.P. do what is minimally required to make it legal, would you still want the marriage? Is it really marriage you want?"

Most couples would answer yes, it's marriage we want. When sitting in a pastor's office people often aspire to be covenantal and good, or at least to look good. If it's mostly the sex they want, they tend not to admit it to clergy.

Oh, admit it. If not to me, then please, to yourselves and each other. This is what I wish I had said to the first couple I ever pronounced husband and wife. Initially they had asked to preside at their marriage the Senior Pastor of the church I was then newly serving in a supporting pastoral role. Knowing as he did the sordid details of the couple's liaison, the elder clergyman begged off and slipped the couple my phone number. I married them six days after I was ordained to the ministry of Word and Sacrament. Preoccupied and green, I hadn't asked enough questions, or the right questions, during my premarital meetings with the couple. Too late did I learn that the bridegroom had recently divorced a local clergywoman with whom he had fathered numerous children, whose former babysitter was his new bride. He left her, too, in a matter of months. It took a bit longer than that for me to gain credibility among a few disgusted neighboring pastors. But then, how could they know I had been set up by a clergy colleague known to joke: "Me? Stressed? Sure, I've been beating my wife, but I wouldn't say I'm stressed." I think of her, that jocular pastor's long-suffering spouse, and the taut soprano laugh she coughed up when he made this remark at a party. I wonder: how many untold grievances has she slept on over the years? Maybe her ability to sleep while angry is the very key to her marriage's endurance.

"Marriage is a boy-girl slumber party for the rest of your life." This is not all I believe marriage to be, but having had no time to prepare my remarks, I said it to a couple of friends, Judd and Justine, before signing the certificate that would legalize their union. "Are you ready?"

They were ready. Theirs remains my favorite of the weddings I've "done," as we say in the business. Judd and Justine had been living together for ten years, in a tiny apartment with a four-poster bed in the living room. Judd's health insurance had recently expired, so he needed to be included on Justine's policy. He had quizzed me about how one might go about getting married, but had never come out and asked me to do any honors. Now, in the company of four unsuspecting friends who had gathered on the patio of Rocco's Little Chicago Pizzeria, he pushed aside a few empty Old Style cans and the crusty remains of the Heart Attack Special. "Well, Reverend," he said, placing a marriage license on the table, "shall we do this thing?"

"You can't be serious," somebody said.

But Judd and Justine were serious, in a beer-and-pizza, spousal benefits, I've-loved-you-for-a-decade kind of way. So I improvised my slumber party homily and some vows for the couple to repeat after me, and we signed our names to their marriage. Rocco came out of the kitchen in his sauce-splattered apron and took a few Polaroids.

I loved this wedding's complete lack of artifice. I loved the way my husband Ken choked up a little as he made a toast, and then paid for dinner, telling Judd, "It's your wedding, man. Put your wallet away."

Perhaps my brother Jonny's wedding to Gayle was a little like Judd's to Justine: cozy, authentic, and priceless. I hope so. More than this, I hope that my brother and his bride will never go to sleep with a grievance against one another, now that they have entered into the slumber party of the rest of their lives.

– Day 26 –
To Follow What Your Tongue Is Saying

Poemen said, "Teach your heart to follow what your tongue is saying to others." He also said, "Men try to appear excellent in preaching but they are less excellent in practicing what they preach."

The Desert Fathers, 81

This week, for the first time, I met the neighbors—Monte, the United Methodist pastor, and Jim, the Southern Baptist pastor, who serve churches near the Presbyterian congregation that I serve. We clergy sat down together in Monte's office to imagine an ecumenical, community worship service to take place on the eve of Thanksgiving.

Midway through the conversation the clergymen asked me to preach at this service. A gentle wave of pleasure and excitement washed onto a shoreline inside me, then receded, leaving behind a frothy row of bubbles, happily popping on the sunny sand of my ego. I had entered into the conversation secretly hoping these guys would invite me to preach the Thanksgiving sermon, even though I knew that agreeing to do so would create extra work for me.

"Keep it to twenty or twenty-three minutes," Jim said.

"Oh, my," I answered. "That's a little longer than I usually preach."

"No one will complain if you go shorter," Monte laughed.

"Most Sundays, I preach thirty to thirty-three minutes," Jim said matter-of-factly.

"Really," I marveled.

Off a nearby shelf, Monte grabbed a large hourglass and plunked it on the table before us. A thin stream of white sand fell through its skinny glass waist and began to accumulate in the lower bulb. He told us a parishioner had given it to him.

"I bring it into the pulpit sometimes," Monte said. "I've even turned it back over midway through the sermon. Everybody groans."

I watched the sands of time spilling inexorably into a little heap, and asked Monte, "How long does it take to empty out?"

"Twenty to twenty-three minutes."

I remarked, "Someone once said the average American adult has an attention span of twelve minutes."

Neither Jim nor Monte responded to this dubious factoid. I continued watching the sand falling, piling, and spreading in its sealed glass world. The image of the draining upper bulb of the hourglass aroused an emptying, anxious sensation in my stomach. For an instant I was Dorothy Gale locked in the tower with the Wicked Witch, whose green hand inverted an oversized hourglass. *You see that?* she demanded. *That's how much longer you've got to be alive.*

I'm frightened, Auntie Em, I thought. But then I snapped to, and my colleagues and I joined hands for a prayer.

Notwithstanding the brief, ominous reverie in my Methodist colleague's office, preaching does not, in fact, frighten me as it once did. Early in my preaching life I had recurring dreams of sermons gone terribly and publicly awry—manuscript pages full of shifting Greek text; the sudden onset of laryngitis; heckling worshipers. My early sermons were, I think, peculiar, but not what you would describe as bad. I began by preaching like the former English major beset by vague, mystical longings that I was. I remember, in those early days, a retired clergyman shaking my hand after worship and kindly saying, "That was a very different take on the Scripture." I instantly knew I had missed the point of the biblical text, and had tried to make it say something it didn't really mean.

"Men try to appear excellent in preaching," Abba Poemen once observed. God knows, in my Reformed tradition, whose adherents affirm the presence of the risen Christ in the Word proclaimed, we take preaching seriously. It is nearly sacramental to us, and we can scarcely imagine a worship service without it, whereas the Eucharist we may celebrate only one Sunday per month. But Abba Poemen values excellent practitioners of the faith more highly than excellent preachers. He urges us to walk our talk: "Teach your heart to follow what your tongue is saying to others." What I appreciate about this advice, because it's true to my experience, is Poemen's implication that preachers learn to live the faith by preaching it.

The words I am given to preach instruct me. Unlike some homileticians who prize extemporaneous talk, I write my sermons in advance. On my computer monitor, on paper, they look like blank verse: rhythmic, unrhymed lines of language, broken at the pauses and breaths. As I compose, I sometimes discover, as if for the first time, the Gospel's outlandish promises and demands, its huge hope. The process of drawing out the essential challenges and blessings of a scriptural text and finding words that will help my congregation hear and enact them converts and convicts me. Sermon preparation teaches me that of which I need perpetual reminding: God is faithful, and so are we called to be. Between the last sermon I preached and the next one I'll write, a thousand interventions occur within me: distractions and temptations, forgettings and failures, such that by the time I sit down to work on next Sunday's message, I've backslid plenty and I realize once again that I'm as dense a disciple as any you're likely to find. The way with words that

I bring to the homiletical task is not holiness; it's an ear for the musicality of American English and a flair for verbal transitions. This is not to say I'm an unusual sinner. I'm a usual sinner. It's just that my job involves preaching most Sundays.

I bring my sermon manuscript with me into the pulpit. I glance at it; it prompts me as I preach; I strive never to read at my congregation, but to speak into their hearing the discoveries I made as I prepared my sermon in solitude. I love the power of carefully chosen words, energetically voiced, to reveal what Christians, including the preacher herself, need to know. For me, this knowing is the heart's grasp of what the mouth made plain; it's the heart's pursuit of what the tongue said, and there is, if we take Poemen at his word, no sin in preaching what your heart may not yet realize. You preach what you surmise to be true, despite your heart's opposing inclinations. You preach even when you feel as frightened as Dorothy Gale and what you really want to do is go back home. Eventually you'll get back home, and there you'll try to teach your heart to practice what your mouth has preached.

By the time Pastor Monte, Pastor Jim, and I concluded our meeting in Monte's office the hourglass's upper bulb had nearly emptied, and a small, sloping dune had formed in the lower bulb. I returned to my own church office to write my message for the coming Sunday. In the blessed, undisturbed afternoon, faced as I was with a bracing parable of Jesus, the last remaining bubbles on the beach of my preacher's ego had disappeared. I looked within myself and saw sand, damper and grittier than that in Monte's hourglass, but not, I am thankful to say, scarlet and scary as the sand in the Wicked Witch's hourglass. The sand inside me seemed to be the same sand into which Jesus had fingered some inscrutable message, millennia earlier, before he told a woman that he would not condemn her. At the keyboard I fingered my sermon into being, and as I did, I discovered the Gospel once again, or it discovered me. It washed over me like a wave, cleaning and exposing the broken, yet-unsanded bits of me.

– Day 27 –
Lose It to Find It

[Abba Anthony said], "Do not trust in your own righteousness, do not worry about the past, but control your tongue and your stomach."

The Sayings of the Desert Fathers, 2

Back in the early 1990s, when I first enrolled in theological seminary, it seemed to me that many of my classmates, cradle Christians, wholesome Midwesterners fresh out of college who yearned to serve the church, were much better suited to ministry than I, whose past the sacrament of baptism had not completely rinsed away. One aspect of my past surfaced when, like all candidates for ordination to the ministry of Word and Sacrament, I underwent required psychological and vocational testing. After several hours of assessment I sat with a psychologist who told me I was trying to control my considerable anger but didn't quite know how. There it was, that old bugaboo.

Controlling your anger, or knowing how on earth to express it, is hard when you've been taught that anger isn't an allowable, legitimate emotion. At fourteen I was a girl so angry about the poisoning effect on my family of my father's alcoholism, so angry that I wasn't permitted to be angry, that I kicked in a door and broke the full-length mirror mounted on it. This was not the first of my furious adolescent outbursts, but it is the one that did me in. The psychiatrist my parents enlisted recommended they commit me to the locked psychiatric ward of the local hospital. Family systems theory, systemic under-standings of addiction—these good things had not yet made their way into suburban psychiatry. Locking up the kid—for seven weeks—was still considered therapeutic.

And to be fair, aspects of my hospitalization were helpful, or at least benign. Although I found demeaning the weekly sessions with the shrink, the hours of adjunctive therapy (other-wise known as arts and crafts, like leather-tooling and ceramic-casting) made me feel constructive and artistic. I created gifts for my mother and father, who, I believed, were punishing me for having acted out, and to whom, therefore, I wanted to prove that my goodness outweighed my badness and rage. Whatever my parents believed about me (if they believed anything in particular—mostly, I suspect, they were baffled by the cunning power of alcohol addiction and an opportunistic psychiatrist), in the inpatient psychiatric ward I found it easy to feel sane.

Comparatively, I was plenty sane. Virtually all the other patients had attempted suicide (which I had never considered) and were now being dosed with myriad sedatives and anti-psychotics. That I was never prescribed so much as an aspirin I take as the psychiatrist's tacit acknowledgment that I wasn't all that crazy. In the inpatient smoking lounge with safety lighters bolted to the wall, one woman, whose bleached hair hung limply from black roots, would shuffle across the linoleum and croak, "Our esteemed doctor made me what I am." I liked her honesty—a virtue absent from alcoholic households like the one from which I found myself taking this strange but not entirely unwelcome breather. I remember liking all the other inpatients, really. Delusional and drugged they may have been, but some realities these pained people saw for exactly what they were.

The other inpatients saw me for the hapless, essentially harmless kid *I* was, who craved love and order to counteract the isolation and chaos that infected my home. My older brother and sister had gone away to college, which had left my anxious mother, drunken father, and me, who had just begun high school. We three were wholly unequipped to diagnose or treat our family's disease. I write freely here about the alcoholism because my father has now enjoyed years of sobriety and both of my parents welcome me to do so. Painful and unnecessary an incarceration as my hospitalization was in many respects, I believe that locking me up in the loony bin was the best my mom and dad then knew how to do, having been advised to do so by a medical expert they had turned to in a panic.

Years after the fact, how do you explain such things to the mental health professional who has been hired to gauge your fitness to serve as a church leader? Well, you just tell him, plainly, without shame but with plenty of prayer that the church will understand that the past is over and gone and a fresh, new life has begun, even for a minister-in-training who can identify just a little with biblical demoniacs, those first-century misunderstood crazies to whom Jesus gave a chance at an unchained life in community. You do roughly what Abba Anthony long ago advised a monk-in-training to do: "Do not trust in your own righteousness, do not worry about the past." Doing my best not to worry, I told my evaluator about my weird history, mentioning as well the far less dramatic counseling I was currently undergoing at the Center for Religion and Psychotherapy. He made a note on a legal pad.

In his written report on my mental state, which my evaluator submitted to the denominational committee charged with overseeing my preparations for ministry, I looked like a young adult coming to grips with the things that still angered her, though no longer to the point of kicking down doors and breaking mirrors. One member of that Presbyterian committee, a fortyish man in a necktie, questioned me about the report's reference to my ongoing psychotherapy, which seemed not to strike him as the good sign it was. Did I imagine the wincing sympathy on the faces of the other committee members as I explained the spiritually healing effects of my weekly counseling appointments? Were some of them—the quietly nodding committee members, especially—possibly people who, like me, had been emotionally wounded by life? Deep in their hearts, did they find, as I found, that the stories of Jesus' healings of people possessed by evil spirits made poignant, undeniable sense?

If such stories make sense to you—if, say, you are one of the roughly nineteen million Americans who suffer from depression—be prepared, if you talk openly about such things, for someone to look at you as if you're crazy. We may be a nation of what I like to call Paxil Achievers, but the social stigma surrounding mental health difficulties, and mental health care, persists. We're not so different from first-century people who attributed mental illness to demons and tried to control the mentally ill by binding them in chains. As a people, we are still sufficiently ashamed of painful emotional struggle that we tend to prefer putting on a brave face to seeking help. We are still mortified when we see someone "losing it."

People were always losing it with Jesus. The demoniacs with whom Jesus dealt had little ability to control their tongues. Abba Anthony (who himself confronted plenty of demons) and other desert monastics were big proponents of silence and self-control. But the tortured souls Jesus met in his travels were anything but silent and self-controlled. They were given to shouting questions like, *What have you to do with us, Jesus of Nazareth?* How quick they were to spot the Messiah in their midst, possibly because, in his way, Jesus, too, was a little touched in the head, and it showed.

Every church has its demoniacs, its unbalanced saints who cause the congregation to blush and remember how close to the edge of sanity we all live. I knew one such Christian who desperately needed, in the words of a psychologist friend, "to put a lid on his id." I watched this man lose the ability to control his impulses and his tongue. I marveled at his vocalized streams of consciousness. He used up my patience and maddened me at times. I wished he would regain his grip, or at least, for the love of God, shut up.

In the middle of one manic monologue in which he both manifested his craziness and spoke of desperately needing help with it, he said he hoped the local hospital would admit him as a patient. "You've got to lose control to get control, you know?"

"No," I told him, sighing, having grown weary of listening, "I don't know."

"Okay, put it this way. You've got to lose your life to find it. Does that make sense to you?"

Startled, chastened, I felt the sense the man was making, and understood his sad hope that he would be deemed sufficiently uncontrolled to receive the care and find the self-control he needed. In a past that now seemed so distant I scarcely remembered or worried about it any longer, I, too, had once lost control. As a furious fourteen-year-old who had emotionally lost it one too many times, I then became a psychiatric inpatient and lost all control over my circumstances, to live for seven weeks in a community of people so anguished most of them had tried to die. It was these very losses, of my temper and my personal freedom—losses made bearable, as I now know they were, by God's love for me—that put me on the winding, truthful path toward what is now my ability to get angry without causing property damage. Call it mental health or a measure of spiritual maturity, call it repression or self-control. Whatever it is, some of us have to lose it to find it.

– Day 28 –

Fighting Fire

Syncletica said . . . "Keep saying the famous text: 'The Lord hath
chastened and corrected me: but he hath not given me over to
death.' Iron is cleaned of rust by fire. . . . Gold is tested by fire."

The Desert Fathers, 64

The late sun, like a woman stylishly battling cancer,
wraps its bald head in a gaudy silken scarf,
but can't prolong the glory of the sunset
or postpone the dusk.
The blackened, mountainous horizon
sinks, as it must,
into rust and shadow, until the west
goes as dark as the east,
and faraway stars
light their cigarettes.
Here it is, the desert day's
denouement, the chill, charcoal night.
At the center of old, encircled rocks,
you prop up a teepee of kindling,
leaving room for air currents

to do-see-do among the dry branches.
You strike a match
and blow like the devil on faint sparks.
They flare into flames that you feed
wadded paper. Yesterday's news
turns into tonight's gassy blues,
its flagrant oranges and golds,
its dancing ghosts, its inky, skyward smoke.

– Day 29 –

In the Stillness, in the Calm

[Abba Paul said], "The peace of the night is enough for us if our thoughts are watchful."

The Sayings of the Desert Fathers, 204

Earlier this week the peace of the night proved insufficient. The thoughts of a young woman named Galareka Harrison were far from watchful. An eighteen-year-old member of the Navajo nation, she had recently enrolled in the First-Year Scholars program of the University of Arizona's Native American Student Affairs Office. Galareka's dormitory roommate, Mia Henderson, also Navajo, also eighteen, was also a First-Year Scholar and a tribal scholarship recipient.

Neither young woman now lives in the dorm. Mia is dead. Galareka, having been arraigned on a charge of first-degree murder, resides in a jail cell. A few days before she died, Mia filed a theft report with the university police, expressing her suspicion that Galareka had stolen items from her purse. This allegedly enraged Galareka to the point where she purchased a knife, forged a suicide note in Mia's name, and at 5:30 a.m. repeatedly stabbed her roommate as she slept.

Within forty-eight hours of Mia Henderson's murder a Navajo medicine man performed a private, solemn cleansing ritual in the dormitory where she had died. Manley Begay, Director of the University of Arizona's Native Nation's Institute for Leadership, told reporters, "Even though we're such a distance from the Navajo Nation, there's still a tremendous amount of caring for our students."[8]

Whereas the University of Arizona is situated in Tucson, in southern Arizona, *Diné Bikéyah,* or Navajo Country, covers 27,000 square miles of desert territory in northeastern Arizona, as well as a part of Utah and a portion of New Mexico at the Colorado border. Several years ago, traveling through this Four Corners region, with its rural poverty, ugly commercial strips, flashy casinos, and the astounding, noiseless beauty of *Tse'Bii'Ndzisgaii,* or Monument Valley, my husband Ken and I discovered that hotel rooms aren't cheap in Navajo Country. So we spent the night at the affordable Rainbow Inn, a student-operated bed-and-breakfast in a converted dormitory of Diné College in Tsaile, Arizona. While traditional hogans (octagonal or hexagonal Navajo dwellings) are constructed of mud-packed logs, the Rainbow Inn is a cinderblock hogan. Our breakfast of cornflakes pointed, vaguely, to the importance of corn in the customary Navajo diet.

"May you always walk the corn pollen trail," wrote an anonymous contributor to an online condolence book intended for the family of Mia Henderson, the murdered Navajo student.[9] Another contributor to the book quoted the Navajo Night Chant:

> Happily I recover.
> Happily my interior becomes cool.
> Happily I go forth.
> My interior feeling cool, may I walk.
> No longer sore, may I walk.
> Impervious to pain, may I walk.
> With lively feelings may I walk.
> As it used to be long ago, may I walk.[10]

Cheryl Jackson of Tuba City, Arizona, the town in which Mia Henderson grew up, wrote of her, "She was among the most gentle and kindest of people, our lady warrior who went off just weeks ago to walk in her beauty, and now she walks with God."[11]

Perhaps because inappropriate content had been deleted, the online condolence book completely lacked negative remarks about Galareka Harrison, Mia's alleged murderer. One contributor named S. Iron Rope wrote, "My heart is saddened to hear of such a tragic event to my Native peoples."[12]

Navajo tribal president Joe Shirley Jr., felt similar sorrow. After learning of Mia's murder he remarked: "Is the culture going away, are we losing the culture? We're all family. We're supposed to be getting along; we're supposed to be looking out for each other. We take care of our own. That's supposed to be the philosophy, the belief, the way."[13]

Traditional Navajo belief emphasizes the four directions. The East, from which dawn arises, is the thinking direction and reminds tribal people to reflect before they act. The South is the planning direction, representing careful mental preparation for action. The West is the living realm, where Navajos realize the thoughts and plans of the East and South. North represents retrospect and evaluation, where the actions of the West and the thoughts and plans of the East and South are assessed, and if necessary, changes are made. Each dawn, arising from the East, offers a new opportunity for watchful thought and, as the Navajo chant expresses it, "walking in beauty."

Navajo watchfulness, to which the night's darkness is prelude, resembles the mindfulness of such ancient desert Christians as Abba Paul, who said, "The peace of the night is enough for us if our thoughts are watchful." Comparably, another early Christian contemplative, Theodoros the Ascetic, advised, "Pray . . . with a watchful and vigilant mind."[14] Whether Egyptian or North American, Christian or tribal, practitioners of desert spiritualities cultivate an honorable life of reverence, simplicity, deep self-awareness, and repentance.

What drove Galareka Harrison so far from such values, to desperate brutality? What madness overtook her thoughts as she allegedly bought a knife and put it to appalling use? Upon learning of her daughter's arrest, Galareka's mother, Janice Harrison, could answer no such questions. A fine-featured woman with her hair neatly pulled back, she was grim but composed as she told a reporter, "She never did anything wrong. She's a real nice person. She's never been away from home. She has no record of anything like this. She wanted to be a pharmacist."[15] Galareka Harrison's bond was set at $50,000. The presiding judge rejected a prosecutor's request that it be raised to $1 million, stating that even the $50,000 would exceed the Harrison family's resources.

Years prior to Mia Henderson's murder, Navajo writer Al Durtschi wrote: "The modern world has almost destroyed the Navajo world. [The] teachings almost disappeared. Our young people have found it difficult to exist in both worlds and some feel like they don't fit in either world."[16] Durtschi's words echo the deep concern for the loss of Navajo culture voiced by tribal president Joe Shirley Jr.

"But now," Durtschi goes on, "we as a people are wiser, and like a relative that has been sick, we are making our culture well again. Like a very old grandfather, it holds the knowledge to take care of the family, the Clan, the Navajo Nation, and Mother Earth. We are very serious about what we are doing. We are gaining a greater respect for our old teachings. For they will take care of us individually and as a people."[17]

Who will transmit the old teachings to Galareka Harrison, the Navajo people's sick young relative, as she awaits her trial? If she is found guilty and sentenced to many years in prison, what chance exists that she will find healing and peace in her cell?

On the Sunday following Mia Henderson's death, a member of my church, with pain apparent in her face, voiced a prayer request on behalf of the Henderson family. The next day Mia was buried in *Tséałnáoztií*, or Sanostee, New Mexico. The Henderson family established a fund, donations to which would enable them to purchase a headstone.

"Be still like the desert shrub," wrote a contributor to the Henderson family's condolence book. "Be calm and you will hear your loved one speak. In the stillness, in the calm, their love resounds."[18]

– Day 30 –

Be Both Mary and Martha

Silvanus said, "I think Mary always needs Martha, and by Martha's help Mary is praised."

The Desert Fathers, 105

Now as they went on their way, he entered a certain village, where a woman named Martha welcomed him into her home. She had a sister named Mary, who sat at the Lord's feet and listened to what he was saying. But Martha was distracted by her many tasks; so she came to him and asked, "Lord, do you not care that my sister has left me to do all the work by myself? Tell her then to help me." But the Lord answered her, "Martha, Martha, you are worried and distracted by many things; there is need of only one thing. Mary has chosen the better part, which will not be taken away from her."

Luke 10:38-42

Early in my Christian life, as a newly baptized young adult reading the gospels, I encountered Mary and Martha of Bethany. At church I also encountered Christian women who with a hint of melancholy described themselves as "Marthas" and said they yearned to be "Marys." These women felt they were mainly doers, earnest workers who craved "the better part"—the time and ability to sit at the Lord's feet and listen to what he was saying.

Unlike these productive women of faith, I, upon meeting Mary of Bethany, immediately identified with her. I considered myself a contemplative who strove not to be distracted by many tasks (if such dreamy self-indulgence as I practiced at the time can be described as striving).

I was a college student living with my fiancé, Ken, inarguably the "Martha" of our relationship, especially in our early years together. Whereas I took out student loans so that I might not have to work excessively while pursuing my studies, Ken always put in as many hours as he could, working as a computer guy while also carrying a full-time academic course load. I needed him to do this, or to put it more precisely, in order to enjoy the luxury of leisure time I depended on Ken to do more than his fair share of the work that sustained us both.

"Mary always needs Martha," said Silvanus of the desert. "By Martha's help Mary is praised."

I know this to be true. I know that contemplatives often depend on activists to prepare the food and lay the table where the Lord might break bread and speak a word of wisdom. Were it not for those Marthas who take care of the practical necessities, the Lord would go hungry until it finally occurred to Marys like me to open a can of beans and pop them into the microwave.

The Marthas of my church (and of many other congregations) do much better than heat canned food. I salute Sandy, a woman of the congregation I serve, which loves to eat well. During the supper where I met the congregation for the first time, everybody gratefully filed past long tables, loading up their plates with fried chicken, potato and macaroni salads, brownies, cookies, and pies—everybody except Sandy, who had coordinated the meal preparations and now hustled around in an apron, replenishing dishes and cleaning up pans. Sandy has a kindred spirit in Ginger, who has a knack for finding bulk food bargains and is energized by cooking for large groups.

It's because of the Sandys, Gingers, and Marthas of the church that I'm able to serve as a Mary, a listener to the Lord in their midst. Virtually every preacher depends on those who unlock church doors, turn on sanctuary lights, brew big pots of coffee, and cut communion bread into bite-sized pieces. Were it not for these faithful doers, makers, and fixers, we preachers would never find time to sit with the Scriptures and hear what the Spirit would have us tell the worshipers. And yet, affirmed though I feel as a contemplative by Jesus' words about Mary's having chosen the better part, I no longer believe as I once did that Mary is superior to Martha. Mary could just as soon be called impractical as attentive. Martha might be distracted, but she sure works hard to offer hospitality. It's only by Martha's help, as Silvanus points out, that Mary is able to practice the contemplative vocation for which she receives praise.

In the fourth century, Silvanus established a monastic community in Scetis, south of Alexandria, Egypt. There, he served as spiritual leader to twelve disciples, later relocating with them to Sinai and then to Gaza. We can reasonably imagine that Silvanus was a contemplative leader who functioned as his monastery's Mary, exemplifying the simplicity, prayerfulness, and wisdom for which Desert Fathers and Mothers are remembered. But his remark about Martha's necessity to Mary suggests that Silvanus understood that his interior peace and instructive ministry depended on his disciples' service as Marthas who could be counted on to prepare meals, take out the trash, and generally maintain the *lavra* (monastic cells clustered around a central church).

Like rivalrous siblings, some of Silvanus' disciples resented the seeming favoritism he showed one member of his community, a calligrapher named Mark. Perhaps the disciples' displeasure echoed Martha of Bethany's complaint to Jesus about his preference for Mary. As Jesus had defended Mary, so Silvanus defended Mark. He told some visitors this story: once Silvanus, needing assistance, had knocked on each of his disciples' cell doors, but only Mark had come to his aid. Silvanus appreciated a helper, a Martha, when he found one.

A retreatant at Silvanus' monastery learned about the need for both contemplation and action when he spent the day reading in his cell but then complained to Silvanus after no meal was delivered to him.

"You are a spiritual man and have no need of this food," Silvanus answered, perhaps with the merest teasing glint in his eyes. "We are carnal, and want to eat, and that is why we work."[19] Silvanus' practical realism provides a healthy corrective to otherworldly, irresponsible spiritualities.

Each person may possess an innate predilection for either contemplative stillness or productive activity. But the point for any individual Christian, according to Silvanus, is not to be all Mary or all Martha. Instead, each of us is called to strike a blended balance of the two. Thus each of us may become a whole person who is both a contemplative and an activist, both a hearer and a doer of God's word.

– Day 31 –
Turn to the Old

A brother asked Abba Sisoes the Theban, "Give me a word," and he said, "What shall I say to you? I read the New Testament and I turn to the old."

The Sayings of the Desert Fathers, 219

Early in this book I described a scheduling snafu that prevented me from keeping my commitment to teach a class on *lectio divina* (holy reading) at a local retreat center. Yesterday the teaching opportunity came around once again, and I enjoyed the privilege of introducing the ancient practice of "breaking open the Word" to eighteen new enrollees in the retreat center's school of spiritual direction. However, to say I introduced the practice is not entirely accurate, because most of the learners were seasoned members of religious communities and had been prayerfully reading sacred Scripture for years. I asked them to comment on their ways of incorporating the Bible into their spiritual disciplines. Several men and women described reading short passages slowly, repeatedly, meditatively, allowing a single word or phrase to focus their awareness of God's personally addressing them and evoking their prayerful response. In other words, they talked about the searching, attentive approach to the Bible that St. Benedict called *lectio divina*, which he taught monks to engage in for a portion of each day.

When I "teach" *lectio divina* to longtime Christian spiritual practitioners I do far less introducing of unfamiliar material than affirming and reinforcing of what they already know. Standing at the head of a classroom full of experienced and committed seekers after God, I sometimes feel as Abba Sisoes must have felt when he said to a brother, "What shall I say to you? I read the New Testament and I turn to the old." I wonder what new material I can possibly convey to people who have been poring over the Scriptures for longer than I have.

Then I remember that the purpose of faithful learning is not always to acquire new knowledge. The better goal may be the development of Christian maturity, the kind I see in many students of *lectio divina* at the school of spiritual direction. These learners represent a blend of knowing and unknowing, expertise and beginner's mind. It takes confidence and humility to claim insights gleaned over years of practice while also maintaining openness to untried perspectives. Sometimes it's enough for Christian adults simply to hear time-tested truths in a new voice. I think of a clergy friend who provides pastoral care to a retired clergywoman old enough to be her grandmother. Recently, addressing a dilemma in the older woman's life, the younger pastor told her, "Everything I'm saying, you already know, and have said to a hundred parishioners yourself."

"I know," the older woman replied. "I just need to hear you say it again."

After Abba Sisoes said, "I read the New Testament and I turn to the old," the monk who had sought a guiding word from him may well have responded, "I know. I just needed reminding."

During a period in my ministry when I rarely preached but often paid visits to the oldest, frailest members of a congregation, at their bedsides I would read aloud the New Testament and then turn to the Old. To be more specific, I would recite with these elders the prayer Jesus taught his disciples, and then

I would turn to the twenty-third Psalm, which even Alzheimer's disease could not wipe from my parishioners' memories. These lifelong Christians did not need strange Scriptures or theological surprises; facing their infirmities in the early twenty-first century was strange and surprising enough. They needed the comforting familiarity of "Our Father who art in heaven," especially as they entered the "valley of the shadow of death."

Before I would visit elderly church members, their adult sons and daughters would sometimes warn me, "Mom won't understand you," or "Dad's very confused." But even bewildered, bedridden men and women rendered largely speechless by dementia seemed awakened and soothed by biblical language recalled from their Sunday School days. Their mouths would move in time with the beloved rhythms of the text as I read it aloud. As they remembered the promises of God, I often heard new nuances in the deeply familiar texts.

Having been raised in an irreligious household without exposure to the Bible, I'm a relative latecomer to the Scriptures, which I started to read in my early twenties. I'll never have the experience of sitting on the floor with the other little kids, hearing a Sunday School teacher reading the story of the great flood while looking at bold illustrations of Noah's big ark packed with pairs of animals, overarched by God's bright, reassuring rainbow. Wonderful though it might have been to go to church as a child, my lack of childhood Christian education has its advantages. Unlike some adults I've met in church, I don't know Bible stories in the ingrained and stale fashion that is the problematic side of memorization. I haven't had to unlearn rote religion in order to develop an adult faith. The Scriptures surprise me all the time. What I'm missing in the way of chapter-and-verse mastery I may make up for with a spirit of discovery that's good for my preaching and teaching.

It's when I'm preparing to preach or teach that I practice *lectio divina* and learn what the Spirit is leading me to help others discover. This is what *lectio* can lead to: the fresh experience of eternally good and challenging news about God. On a first or second reading, a sacred text's words may seem old and unremarkable, but as St. Benedict and one of his predecessors, Abba Sisoes, understood, Scripture's words are living and active, able to enter a mind, penetrate a heart, change a life.

When a brother approached Abba Sisoes and asked him for a word, it may have been a new, previously unheard, life-changing word that he sought. Abba Sisoes had nothing new to say; in fact, his brief remark about his reading habits concluded with the words "turn to the old." For one with ears to hear it, this is advice enough. Turn to the old. Turn the pages of the Old and New Testaments and read them searchingly, as if for the first time. Turn to elders like Abba Sisoes, or to venerable, vulnerable churchmen and churchwomen. They may have forgotten what they said five minutes ago, but they know their Bible by heart and are sure to dwell in the house of the Lord their whole lives long.

– Day 32 –
All Eye

When he was dying, Bessarion said, "A monk ought to be like the Cherubim and Seraphim, all eye."

The Desert Fathers, 119

One week before my forty-third birthday, during the sharing of joys and concerns at church, my husband announced, "I give thanks that you were born, and your birthday's next week."

"Yes," I said, a little startled that Ken had revealed my coming birthday to the entire congregation. "I'll be turning forty-three, and what I really want for my birthday is bifocals. I'm starting to play trombone." I moved my worship bulletin up and back before my face, pantomiming that focusing gesture we start to make in middle age.

The next week, during the announcements that precede the worship service, several women of the church surprised me by wheeling down the sanctuary's center aisle a cart bearing a birthday cake that—thankfully—bore only five or six burning candles. The congregation stood and sang to me. I encouraged all of them to join the choir. One woman handed me a gift bag, and out of it I pulled an enormous pair of pink-framed costume glasses. Each plastic lens bore a strip of yellow rickrack across the middle. Now that I had my "bifocals," I dutifully modeled them, to the amusement of the worshipers. Next month, when my insurance allows, I'll see the ophthalmologist—perhaps a bit more clearly after he upgrades my prescription. For my actual progressives (bifocals in disguise), I'll pick out some good-looking frames. If you have to wear hardware on your face, I figure it ought to be attractive.

I'd prefer 20-20 vision like Ken's. (He recently surprised the eye doctor by easily reading line after line of tiny type on the eye chart, and then, Curious George that he is, spent the remainder of his appointment quizzing the doctor about the mysterious equipment that measures other people's faulty eyesight.) Even so, I know I'm fortunate to require only relatively mild corrective lenses, and to have insurance that will pay for them. I'm more privileged than those who receive old glasses from donors to the Lions' Club.

As the faintly blurred edges of these very words betray the obsolescence of the glasses I'm currently wearing, nevertheless, I can see well enough to read, and for this I must pause and give thanks.

Yesterday I met with a woman who can see, but no longer well enough to read. All her life she has read, hungrily, closely. She holds a doctorate in history and has written several books. When she greeted me yesterday, one lens of her glasses bore a darkening patch. "Greetings from your friendly neighborhood pirate," she said.

We sat across from one another in her sunlit study, sipping ice water. She described her grief at the loss of her vision as a hardened ball in her belly that she had to carry with her wherever she went. Clasping her hands in front of her, she likened this grief to that she had felt following her hysterectomy years earlier. We both noted the abdominal location of her pain, and I asked if she thought that, despite the grievous nature of her diminishing vision, there might be any birth to come from the burden she was bearing. "I've made at least twenty-seven phone calls," she told me, and bemoaned her fruitless efforts to penetrate bureaucracies intended to serve people with visual impairments. She needed someone who could read aloud for her the academic texts that were her intellectual lifeblood. She didn't need a radio station that broadcast volunteers reading *USA Today*.

"I thought I might be able to knit," she told me. "I was going to knit you a purple shawl, but my knitting looked like the work of a spider on LSD."

I told her about a woman I had worked for years before, during the year between my undergraduate and graduate studies in the discipline of English. "She'd been blinded," I said, "by her ex-husband. He ritually beat her until she finally managed to leave him. Now she was writing about it. And she was suing him."

"She was a writer?" my companion said, leaning forward, anxious to hear how a kindred soul had managed. "How did she cope with the loss of beauty?"

What a beautiful question it was, full of honesty, sadness, and hope. I remembered my blind employer, who had paid me rather well to read and critique her manuscripts, transcribed from tape recordings, and to coach her in the art of revision, which any writing teacher will tell you means "seeing again." How she coped with the loss of visual beauty (or ugliness, for that matter) was to see again, by means of memory, imagination, and language, the life she had lived before going blind, divorcing, changing her name, reinventing herself. She actively, literarily refused to relinquish her visionary capacities to the man who had ruined her eyes.

My conversation partner nodded, taking in the story, looking to me nothing like a pirate, despite her eye patch. I watched her uncovered eye blinking and darting, observant and alert as any fully sighted eye. She reminded me of what a dying fourth-century monastic named Bessarion had said: "A monk ought to be like the Cherubim and Seraphim, all eye."

Tradition has it that Bessarion had owned only a tunic and a cloak (both of which he gave away, to clothe a dead beggar and a naked man, respectively) and a book of the Gospels (which he sold to redeem a prisoner from slavery). Having stripped himself of all protections and possessions, by the end of his life Bessarion seems to have become one of the ministering spirits to which he compared the ideal monk by alluding to the cherubim and seraphim of Revelation 4:8:

> And the four living creatures, each of them with six wings, are full of eyes all around and inside. Day and night without ceasing they sing, "Holy, holy, holy, the Lord God the Almighty, who was and is and is to come."

The eye-patch-wearing woman with whom I sat, discussing what had been, what was, and what would one day come, had not, I was convinced, lost sight of beauty. She cannot read these printed words, but when I read them to her she will perhaps see herself as I see her: twice as watchful as most people with twice her visual acuity. "Instead of reading," she told me, "I've been staring at my desert tortoise. He'll have to hibernate soon, and I'm going to miss him."

In certain hot months I have seen this desert tortoise, whose favorite foods include romaine lettuce and strawberries. Throughout the desert winter, like some reptilian monk, he hides away in a cave where only God can see him. My friend will miss the tortoise when he's out of sight. But she's in the habit of looking forward—to next spring, to the next thing she'll do. Though her partial blindness is forcing the revision of her life, it will also bring to birth new visions and unimagined beauty:

> as it is written, "What no eye has seen, nor ear heard, nor the human heart conceived . . . God has prepared for those who love God." (1 Corinthians 2:9)

– Day 33 –

What We're Made Of

Hyperichius said . . . "Hollow out the rocky places of your heart, so that you turn them into springs of water."

The Desert Fathers, 161

In the lukewarm municipal indoor pool where I do my water aerobics, other swimmers, many of them recovering from surgeries or living with disabilities, float around with the aid of "noodles"—bendable, brightly-colored foam cylinders. A woman I know was gently exercising in this pool a few weeks after her surgeon pinned her broken hip back together, when a widower paddled up and invited her to go with him to Mexico for Christmas. With its half-naked swimmers in water nearly as warm as the human body, the pool can be a sexy place, especially for senior citizens who seem to go instantly from stiffened to supple when they swim, and for bent and broken people whom the water makes graceful and buoyant as swans. While some swimmers chat with one another in the pool, I tread water and eavesdrop.

"We're sixty-five percent water," I recently heard a flirtatious man tell a floating woman.

"Mm-hm," she replied, lying back, closing her eyes behind the glasses she hadn't removed before climbing into the deep end.

117

I treaded on, enjoying my legs' watery sensations of resistance and support. But I also felt a little regretful because another woman and I had exchanged tense words in the locker room. It had begun when I moved the open door of her locker to gain access to my own.

"Am I in your way, I take it?" she asked me. I had seen her at the pool many times before, but we had never spoken.

I looked her squarely in the face. Crepey lids hooded her blue eyes and she wore an old-fashioned swim cap with a chin strap. Some especially hardened little facet of the thirty-five percent of me that isn't fluid and flowing retorted, "Was that remark really necessary?"

"It was just a question," she said.

"No," I persisted, "it wasn't just a question."

Two seconds later, I was sorry I hadn't simply apologized for encroaching on the public space the old woman took to be her territory. My heart is part flesh, part water, and like some people's kidneys, part stone. My heart contains what a Desert Christian named Hyperichius called "rocky places." Therefore I sometimes say things that make a situation harder and rockier than it has to be.

"Do you want me to move?" the woman asked me.

"No," I said, turning away from her, feeling ridiculous as I pulled down my underpants and stepped into my swimsuit.

Now here I was, bobbing in waters that should have been rounding off the edges of the troubles and pebbles that surface from within me in the course of a day. Yet I avoided the gaze of the old woman in the swim cap despite the fact that she and I were made mostly of the same juices. The underwater half of me kicked like a frog as I listened in on human voices bouncing wetly off the pool's concrete deck and tiled walls.

"I'm in the mood for catfish," the flirtatious man told the floating woman wearing glasses. "You hungry?"

She lifted up her dripping head. Looking freshly baptized, she smiled and said, "I could be."

I lost track of their conversation after that. I wonder: Did she join the man for dinner? And did he glide like a catfish into the hollowed-out springs of her heart?

The desert where I live is naturally a place of few springs. One exception on the east side of Tucson is Agua Caliente Park. There, warm water bubbles up from the rocky, mustard-colored earth and palm trees ring a reservoir where ducks congregate. Maybe Hyperichius, the Desert Christian, had in mind such an oasis when he likened the hard human heart to ground from which water will spring if you dig deep enough and remove the debris.

Toward the end of a day that has tightened my shoulders and threatened to petrify me on the inside, swimming in water as warm as my own blood works on me as Moses, full of the Lord, worked on that rock at Meribah in the book of Numbers:

> Thus you shall bring water out of the rock for them; thus you shall provide drink for the congregation and their livestock. (20:8)

Once, when a church administrator asked me to tell a group of clergy about my spiritual practices, I made a show-and-tell presentation in which I displayed the Rule of St. Benedict and a pair of swimming goggles. While neither of these props would seem to say much about Presbyterian ministry, they represented bodies—of Christ and of water—that support and envelop me, filling my buckets and then some with living waters by which I try to provide drink for my congregation.

Had a parishioner of mine overheard the rude locker room exchange between the swim-cap-wearing woman and me, I would have been properly embarrassed. After all, at my church I've been known to preach such counsel as the psalmist who sang, "O that today you would listen to his voice! Do not harden your hearts, as at Meribah . . ." (Psalm 95:7-8). I fail, sometimes, to practice what I preach or to listen for the voice of God, speaking through unlikely mouths into the ear of my heart. Intolerant and petty though the words, "Am I in your way, I take it?" seemed when I heard them, they came from an old woman who'd probably been brushed aside and made invisible one too many times. This dawned on me in the pool that afternoon as I crossed its clear and peopled water, kicking and working against the very element I'm made of.

– Day 34 –
What Can I Say?

A brother said to Abba Theodore, "Speak a word to me, for I am perishing," and sorrowfully he said to him, "I am myself in danger, so what can I say to you?"

The Sayings of the Desert Fathers, 76

It was late in Lent, and I received a phone call from Joan, the adult daughter of Dorothy, an elderly woman with whom I had ministered two churches ago. It had been two years since I had resigned from the staff of Dorothy's church. When a pastor leaves a church it is understood that she will cease to relate with its members. Dorothy's church had a Senior Pastor, and a staff member responsible for coordinating congregational care. But here was Dorothy's daughter on the phone, imploring me to visit her mother in the care facility where she now lived, beset by grief and dementia.

Dorothy and her husband, Bill, were among the first people to whom I had paid a visit soon after joining the pastoral staff of their church. I remember perching on the edge of a velveteen-upholstered couch in their living room, paging through an album of photos and clippings from their Air Force days. They had been stationed in tropical places, and had sought to serve their country faithfully. Here was a fading image of an earnest, unlined Dorothy in a crisp cap, smiling by a serviceman's bed-side. There was Bill—lean, uniformed, standing at attention on a tarmac.

I never quite pieced together just what Bill had undergone during the war, though he told me the story more than once. His voice would go so soft before giving way to weeping, all I could make out was that there had been an emergency, and only by the inscrutable grace of God had Bill survived, while his buddies had gone down in flames. Dorothy, too, spoke under her breath, even when the situation didn't require it. Bill and Dorothy seemed like secret-keepers who invited me into their confidence. But I never quite caught their whispered meanings.

Bill underwent multiple heart surgeries until the risks out-weighed the potential benefits, and he finally opted to enter into hospice care at the V.A. hospital. I remember praying by his bedside with Dorothy and a kindly chaplain who had showed up. In the middle of the Lord's Prayer, I forgot the words—*bread? debts? temptation?*—and stammered around until we finally got to *forever and ever.*

Later, driving away from the hospital down the entrance ramp to the highway, I misjudged the distance between my car's fender and some collapsible construction barricades and sent them crashing to the concrete. Shaken, I drove to the des-ert retreat center where I had arranged to spend the afternoon reading and writing. I inspected the damage to my car, then sat amid the sunlit quiet of the place, wondering what was wrong with me. I had provided plenty of pastoral care to the dying and their families. Why was I coming undone today? The answer seemed to be a secret, something whispered I couldn't quite make out, and still can't.

After Bill died, Dorothy asked me to write a poem and read it at his funeral, which took place the day before Easter. Such a request is a challenging thing. You really have to get it right. I hope I did.

Your Whole Life

In death,
your long, reluctant letting go,
you took, then finally gave away, your breath,
and in this giving, your living was made whole.
Dying, on the face of it, was unlike you,
out of character, a mystery
to which your seeming immunity had lasted
through eighty-five years and one world war.

How young you were when you flew
low over that occupied, erupting European theater,
which was no theater at all, but appallingly real.
You watched boys your own age
whose names and faces became forever
imprinted in the pages of your memory, fall
to their premature and violent ends.

Somehow, for some reason, you were spared,
carried home in one piece, astounded, still young,
now infused with a deep sense of duty
and a reverence so tender you could scarcely
whisper God's name without tears.

You now knew your life, like every life,
was one unrepeatable miracle,
and that faithfulness demanded you live it
long and lovingly and well.

Your duty is today fulfilled.
For the rest of us, this is still Holy Saturday,
a grave and watchful interim.
We must be vigilant. Confronted as we are
by the strangeness of new grief, we must struggle
to believe that no tomb—
not yours, not Christ's, not ours—
can forever enclose you, or Jesus, or us.

But resurrection-faith in the face of contrary evidence
is no longer your dilemma.
For you, the wait is over.
It is already Easter for you, eternally Easter.
Reluctant though you were to leave here,
reluctant though we were to let you go,
we need you now as you are:
whole and holy,
your duty done, your faith fulfilled,
your heart wide open, welcoming as heaven.

Grief engulfed Dorothy after Bill died. Life lost all its luster and meaning. Dorothy broke both hips, went almost entirely deaf, and ceased to distinguish the past from the present, the real from the imagined. At the same time that she was entering into dementia, I was leaving behind the church where I had known her. I was surprised when her daughter Joan, who lived in another state but was staying temporarily in Arizona to be close to her mother, tracked me down by phone two years later.

"Maybe you can say something to Mother," Joan told me. "Maybe you can tell her it's all right, she can go now. Maybe she'll believe it, coming from a pastor."

The desert towns and cities of Southern Arizona are home to many older Americans, who move here after deciding never again to shovel snow. When they grow very old, when they lie dying, their adult children, who live and work and have families somewhere "back east," come to Arizona, where they know no one. Although many of these adult children have no religious affiliation of their own, they suddenly rely on their parents' pastors to see them through their family crisis and their loss.

But I was no longer Dorothy's pastor. She had a pastor, but her daughter didn't trust him, and she didn't want him at her mother's deathbed. Deciding that the needs of the dying and the living who love them must supersede questions of pastoral territory, I agreed to visit Dorothy.

I eventually got there—to Dorothy's hospice room—but first I found myself delaying the visit, occupied as I was with caring for my new congregation, and pressured as I had felt by Joan to say some magical, mystical words that would enable Dorothy to die serenely.

"I myself am in danger, so what can I say to you?" Abba Theodore asked this of the perishing brother who sought a word of wisdom from his desert elder. Surely every hospice chaplain, every pastor or deacon or simply concerned friend has felt at just such a loss for words when faced with a dear, dying person. I felt sad and privileged and at best semi-adequate as I looked for the last time into Dorothy's now sunken, shadowy face. She lay in a narcotic-induced sleep while her son slumped nearby in a chair, staring at nothing in particular. At one point he blew his nose and told me that his mother had recently said to him, "You got me into this, you get me out, even if you have to kill me."

I smoothed Dorothy's hair and talked to her—although she surely couldn't hear me—about how God would soon be welcoming her home. I even bade her a safe journey, which frankly sounded a little strange to me as I said it, but I decided not to worry about that, and then I prayed aloud in words that must have been of God's own providing because, as I entered into the prayer, I felt myself teetering on a brink, a precipice beyond which lay ineffable mystery. I refrained from saying the Lord's Prayer, lest my memory fail me.

When I opened my eyes after saying the final "amen," Dorothy's eyes were still closed, but the circles around them had lessened enough that I was startled by the change in her appearance. There was light in her face now, and she looked almost pleased, as though she'd remembered a secret. What the secret was, I couldn't guess and still can't.

– Day 35 –
Velvet Ash

In that place when Ephraim of holy memory was a boy, he saw in sleep, or by revelation, that a vine was planted on his tongue and it grew and filled the whole earth with very great fruitfulness and so all the birds of the air came and ate the fruits of that vine and spread the fruit further.

The Desert Fathers, 187

At the center of my parents' backyard in Albuquerque, New Mexico, stands a grand old Velvet Ash tree with ridged and furrowed gray bark. Provided they get enough water, Velvet Ash trees thrive in the brilliant sunshine and alkaline soil of the desert. From my parents' family room window, the Velvet Ash is the first thing you see, shading the feeders where hummingbirds and sparrows eat. The tree's lanceolate leaves go bright gold in autumn and then crisply carpet the ground. When my nephews were little, a children's swing hung from the tree's thickest bough. Several years later, the tree developed Ash Yellows, a disease that can cause various symptoms including the formation of witches-brooms at the trunk's base. But the tree's dieback was minimal, and thanks be to God, it's still standing.

The Velvet Ash reminds me of a tree that didn't grow in the Chicagoland backyard of my childhood, except in a dream. I was about eight years old and undergoing a brief but potent mystical awakening. One morning during this period I dreamed that in the center of our backyard a great tree had suddenly grown. It held amazing promise: shadows and stability, hiding places, birdsong and birds' nests, berries and breezes, branches to climb, sturdy elevations from which to consider the world. In my pajamas I rushed to the kitchen window to confirm the magnificent tree was truly rooted in the backyard. It wasn't. The morning, like so many mornings in Chicagoland, was gray, and where the tree should have been there was only a ragged dirt path in the grass, formed by our beloved family dachshund, who would run up and back, barking and crapping. Actual, unremarkable trees stood in their usual places: the elm with an octagonal bench built around it, a cherry sapling near the tomato bed. With a little lurch of hope I crossed the house and went to the dining room window. In the front yard the big sickly crab apple tree whose bruised fruit always smelled like alcoholic cider had neither died nor sprung to miraculous new life.

"It came into being in a night and perished in a night," said God of the shade tree that comforted the pouty prophet Jonah east of Tarshish (Jonah 4:10). My tree lasted no longer than Jonah's, and my disappointment was perhaps no less bitter than his. Jonah was "angry enough to die," and sometimes, as a child, so was I. But I did have a rich inner life. In the middle of such homely tasks as loading breakfast plates into the dishwasher I would experience an invisible, living presence I later concluded was God, trying to get my attention despite my irreligious upbringing. For a time during my childhood, with no external encouragement, I sought to know God. I felt—as I pray all children may feel—that a holy life was in me, moving through me as tree sap moves through branches and stems. Sometimes I felt blessed and called and gifted, as "Ephraim of holy memory" must have felt as a boy, when he dreamed a great, life-giving vine had sprouted from his tongue.

As a child, surreptitiously, I clipped the Lord's Prayer from a discarded Christmas greeting sent to my parents by some churchy acquaintance. I quietly recited it at night. But just as my dream of the glorious tree had been fruitless, so, it seemed, was my undercover, bedtime spiritual discipline, and pretty soon I quit praying and the kitchen theophanies stopped.

A grown-up can wander in an inner wilderness, thirsty and lost, and so can a child, whose yearnings for God go unwatered, find herself in a spiritual desert. Children need a faith community to cultivate their growth in God. There is a six-year-old boy who calls the pale earthen-tinted building where our Christian congregation gathers "the pink church." As he shows me the picture he drew in Sunday School, he tells me, "I like it here."

"I like it here, too," I tell him, and I think we both like it here for the same reasons: there's lemonade and living water here and we grow here.

In a family that never went to church, I did grow as a child, but to extend the botanical metaphor, in adolescence I grew into a cactus of a girl, of the Strawberry Hedgehog variety. I was plump but thoroughly barbed, able to produce beautiful blossoms and sugary fruit but not without scratching you first. It took years, a strong marriage, many hours of worship, stacks of books about sacred things, good teachers, and a pilgrimage deep into an actual desert for me to become spiritually deciduous, rooted and grounded in love, capable of turning over new leaves.

Nowadays, when I visit my parents in their desert home and look out into their backyard, I see bright daylight, a grapevine-draped gazebo, a bank of Jumping Cholla camouflaging the compost bin. I see a small rock-bordered pond and a "Beware of Frog" sign near a pomegranate tree. I see the cement grave marker that my mother decorated and placed in loving memory of a pet cat, and the garden patch where my father coaxes succulent peppers to grow. At the center of it all, overlooking everything, stands the rough and silvery-barked Velvet Ash tree, its one-winged seeds like tiny green helicopter blades, its boughs asymmetrical but stronger for the ministrations of the local arborist.

– Day 36 –
Learn, Then Teach

A hermit said, "I would rather learn than teach."

The Desert Fathers, 167

One day my husband Ken and I received in the mail a tastefully designed invitation. On the front it bore a spare illustration of Midwestern grasses and a poem, "air/for one," by Ralph J. Mills, Jr. I suspected what the card would say inside, but I didn't want to confirm my suspicions right away. So I lingered over the poem, as Ralph had taught me to do. "Air, / for one, /takes your place," the poem said, and I knew with a sad pang that air had taken Ralph's place. Ken and I, who had been two of Ralph's writing students twenty years earlier, were invited to a celebration of his life. How remarkable, I thought, that his family had looked us up.

In the spring of 1987, at the University of Illinois at Chicago (UIC), Ken and I met and flourished in the Intermediate Poetry Writing workshop Ralph taught. That semester, when I would sit down to write, whether on a public bus or in my apartment, the poetic experience startled me. As a line of words would form on the paper in front of me, as I named things and weighed the pauses between lines and stanzas, I felt enlarged and transformed, as though I had taken a step so big my right foot had landed with a crunch on the bright, calcium moon. Like every other student in Ralph's class, I would distribute copies of my poems for the students to "workshop." Because Ken was always recommending radical revisions of students' poems, Ralph nicknamed him "the surgeon."

One day after class I turned to Ken and said, "You never say anything about my poems."

"I *like* your poems," he told me, and it was so good to hear, the classroom suddenly seemed too public a place for what either of us might say next.

At the end of the semester Ralph asked the students to complete the customary course evaluations, which two students were required to deliver, unread, to the English Department. Ken and I volunteered. On our way to University Hall we sat cross-legged on the grass under one of the campus's few trees. Our knees bumped. We opened the envelope and read the evaluations aloud to one another, cracking up and discarding those that weren't wholly complimentary of Ralph. We delivered the rest to the Department, including Ken's, which concluded, "Give the Dr. a raise!"

Among the university's Creative Writing faculty (which included Allen Ginsberg's early publisher, the poet Paul Carroll, who, late in his career, would sit in his office breakfasting on toast and Miller beer), only Ralph held a doctorate, which impressed us. He'd practiced literary criticism long before he published any poetry, though in the end his poetry books outnumbered his collections of critical essays. A few hours after Ken and I received word of Ralph's death we went to a wood-fired pizza place we like called Amore Vero and clinked wine glasses: "To Ralph J. Mills, Jr." We remembered how his wedding gift to us had been the third edition of *Benet's Reader's Encyclopedia*.

By speaking with unpretentious authority on the works of many contemporary writers, Ralph taught us to read, closely and widely. By writing skinny, exquisitely attentive poems about his backyard's flora, he taught us to observe the world and to love words, their breath and heft and the spaces and relationships between them. He modeled for us unsentimental ways to think and talk about poetry, and helped us, therefore, to write smarter, more honest and musical poems. And yet, much as he was our teacher, Ralph, like an unnamed desert hermit of the fourth or fifth century, might well have said, "I would rather learn than teach." He surely preferred studying starlings picking blue fruits from a vine to discussing student writing, which ranged from promising to weak to atrocious.

At UIC, when he wasn't in the classroom, discussing diction or line breaks, Ralph was often quietly griping to insiders about misguided department chairmen and even more dangerous deans. As the English Department's computer guy, Ken was an insider, and by extension, so was I. In remembrance of Ralph, Joel Felix, editor and publisher of the Chicago-based journal, *LVNG*, wrote, "He could talk about how the ice storms in Chicago had changed, the ice pellets themselves incrementally more full of grit, in a way that felt like his imagination was turned away from other dynamics, then change subject to the swiftly decaying culture of the university."[20]

How Ralph withstood thirty years of teaching at UIC, with its infamous architectural follies of crumbling cement, its many underprepared students and disaffected faculty, is a puzzle. Ralph was a noticer of such minute details as grit in ice pellets. Three decades at UIC could have frozen or ground down his powers of observation, but didn't. Probably Ralph noticed Ken and me falling in love with each other in his class before we realized it ourselves. After we both placed in a university-wide poetry contest, we participated in a public reading at which Ralph was present. Ken, apparently having become aware of his feelings, announced that one of his previously untitled poems, a draft of which we had critiqued in Ralph's class, was called "Rachel." Seated beside my then-boyfriend, Curt, I was thunderstruck, but Ralph could not have been surprised. Early in his own writing career he had dedicated a poem called "You" to his wife, Helen: "When you step through a door /in your hair

/an edge of fire bites the darkness/ . . . Touching your breast I /think I can't grow old."[21]

Ralph did grow old, and eventually died, in the words of Helen Mills, "gently, mercifully, in his sleep."[22] I look at a photo Helen took of a handsome, pensive Ralph when he was the age I am now, an age Ken has a couple years yet to reach. I think of how, on occasion, Ken and I still dare to doubt we can grow old. But as we approach a double-digit wedding anniversary, the fourth edition of *Benet's Reader's Encylopedia*, which was published several years after we married, is over a decade old. Having been tenured for a few years now, Ken looks toward full professorship, and I am solo-pastoring a church comprised of many retired adults. The possibility of our eventual old age is harder to deny than it once was.

We are both of us teachers—Ken, of the discipline called Rhetoric, and I, of the mysteries and practicalities of faith. When we're feeling overburdened by responsibilities, or nostalgic, or both, sometimes, we would rather learn than teach. Sometimes we would rather live as a pair of studious desert hermits than as public people helping others learn the ways of language or live the ways of Jesus. But teaching the arts of persuasion and the truths of the Gospel is the work for which our teacher helped prepare us, by urging us to care deeply for words and their effects. By turning toward us what Denise Levertov called his "clearest of clear eyes," Ralph Mills taught Ken and me to look and listen, write and speak, teach and preach, authentically and clearly.

– Day 37 –

And Have Not Love

A brother, being tempted by a demon, went to a hermit and said,
"Those two monks over there live together sinfully." But the hermit
knew that a demon was deceiving him. So he called the brothers
to him. In the evening [the hermit] put out a mat for them, and
covered them with a single blanket, and said, "They are sons of
God, and holy persons." But he said to his disciple, "Shut this
slandering brother up in a cell by himself; he is suffering from the
passion of which he accuses them."

The Desert Fathers, 43

When I was an unchurched young adult, just venturing into
Christian congregational life, longtime women of faith invited
me to Bible study. Men of the church welcomed my boyfriend
and me to potlucks and church meetings. As we became involved in this hospitable community of urban Presbyterians,
Ken and I realized that many of its most effective evangelists
were gay. Sandy and Dawn were a faithful couple who remained
friends with Sandy's ex-husband, the congregation's tireless
treasurer. Matt, a man who could prepare pasta puttanesca
for one hundred without breaking a sweat, combined liturgical
artistry and playful bitchiness. He set the vocal standard for
the choir's tenors and teased his friends at coffee hour. At our

wedding, he sang 'The Gift of Love' with such sincerity and dignity that its lyric, based on 1 Corinthians 13, remarkably sounded not the least bit clichéd. Nor did he express a hint of annoyance about the fact that had he wanted to marry the love of his life, neither the law of the land nor the law of the church would have permitted it.

Along with other gay church members and their straight allies, Matt worked to change both civil and ecclesiastical laws so that gay, lesbian, bisexual, and transgender people would enjoy the same rights as heterosexuals. But everyone's participation in the congregation's life was first an expression of Christian disciple-ship, not sexual politics. Since I was baptized at age twenty-three in this church, roughly one-third of whose members were gay, my early adult Christian formation emphasized an image of Jesus as the liberator of oppressed and marginalized people, and the dismantling of all prejudices, including homophobia, as manifes-tations of God's reign of peace, love, and justice on earth.

In 1996, forty years after women gained the right to serve as ministers of the Word and Sacrament in the branch of the Presbyterian Church to which I belonged, I decided to pur-sue ordination. That same year, the General Assembly of the Presbyterian Church (USA) approved an amendment to its constitution, stating: "Those called to office in the church are to lead a life in obedience to Scripture and in conformity to the confessional standards of the church. Among these stan-dards are to live in fidelity within the covenant of marriage between a man and a woman, or chastity in singleness. Persons refusing to repent of any self-acknowledged practice which the confessions call sin shall not be ordained and/or installed as deacons, elders, or ministers of the Word and Sacrament."[23] With the passage of this amendment the Presbyterian Church (USA) entered into a period of polarization and unease that continues more than ten years later.

Nevertheless, Presbyterian ministry in Jesus' name and to God's glory continues, too. One year after the passage of the

Presbyterian "fidelity and chastity amendment," I served as a student pastoral intern for a small, working-class congregation in Chicago. Its members did what Christians do: worshiped and praised their Creator, and in the name and manner of their Lord, empowered by the Holy Spirit, cared for one another as well as for their local and global neighbors. To put it more concretely, the congregation gathered on Sundays to sing and pray, eat coffee cake and chat. They provided a meeting place for and participated in community policing and Twelve-Step groups. They sent money to worldwide missions and collected bedding for nearby homeless shelters. They honored the dead, proclaimed the resurrection, and delivered casseroles to the bereaved. They did all of this undeterred by the fact that their pastor was a lesbian, albeit one practicing "chastity in singleness."

I'm with Peter Gomes, author of numerous books and Pastor and Professor at Harvard University. In an article entitled "Homophobic? Re-Read Your Bible," Gomes writes:

> The same Bible that anti-feminists use to keep women silent in the churches is the Bible that preaches liberation to captives and says that in Christ there is neither male nor female, slave nor free. And the same Bible that on the basis of an archaic social code of ancient Israel and a tortured reading of Paul is used to condemn all homosexuals and homosexual behavior includes metaphors of redemption, renewal, inclusion and love—principles that invite homosexuals to accept their freedom and responsibility in Christ and demand that their fellow Christians accept them as well.[24]

Elsewhere Gomes has remarked: "We have watched the prejudice against women addressed and transformed; the same against Jews, and the same against racial minorities. Logic suggests that this last prejudice [homophobia] will meet that same fate."[25]

Homophobia's history is long. I pray its future will not be. With many other Christians I affirm Peter Gomes's prediction that this "last prejudice" will be addressed and transformed by those in and beyond religious institutions committed to the full inclusion of all people. Frankly, the teachings of the Desert Fathers and Mothers are unlikely to lend much wisdom to such efforts. Warren Johansson and William A. Percy, historians of sexuality, note: "The Desert Fathers increased sexual negativism of other Christians just as monasticism emerged and heightened the temptations of homosex for the cloistered."[26]

Desert monastics struggled to overcome what they deemed the demons of lust and fornication and, like other early Christians, were profoundly influenced by the homophobic mores of ancient Hellenistic and Jewish cultures. Pachomius (a founder of desert monasticism) "said that 'no monk may sleep on the mattress of another' or come closer to another 'whether sitting or standing' than one cubit (about 18 inches) even when they took meals together."[27] But then there is the story of a desert hermit, apparently quite willing to defy Pachomius' prohibition on same-sex bedfellows, who covers two sleeping "sons of God and holy persons" with a single blanket. In every age there have been such compassionate, nonjudgmental Christians. And in every Christian congregation there are faithful gay people like Matt, who sang at our wedding:

> Though I may speak with bravest fire,
> And have the gift to all inspire,
> And have not love, my words are vain,
> As sounding brass, and hopeless gain.[28]

(Words by Hal Hopson ©1972 Hope Publishing Co., Carol Stream, IL 60188. All rights reserved. Used by permission.)

– Day 38 –

Her Own Heart

Antony said, "He who sits alone and is quiet has escaped from
three wars: hearing, speaking, seeing: but there is one thing against
which he must continually fight: that is, his own heart."

The Desert Fathers, 8

Some years ago, soon after I was hired to serve as Director
of Compassion Ministries for a multi-staff church, the Office
Manager gave me a list of solitary senior citizens to call on. I
arranged to visit a woman named June in her home. She was
in her eighties and her husband had died some thirty years
earlier. Her tidy living room appeared to have been furnished
back when he was still living. June and I sat tentatively, facing
one another in boxy, mustard-colored chairs.

"June," I asked, "how long have you been a member of our
church?"

I was surprised when she told me it had been only two
years. She looked abstractly toward the window, with its layered beige draperies, and I decided to probe a little. "Was there
another church before this one?"

"There was," she said crisply. "I went there for years, but
I left two and a half years ago, after my daughter went and
died on me." June looked straight at me and began to speak

of how she'd cared for her daughter "until the cancer finally won. Barbara was a nurse, you know, but then I wound up nursing her. In the end, she couldn't even go to the bathroom on her own. I had to do it for her, pull it out of her. You can't imagine."

"No, I don't think I can," I said.

"After the funeral, nobody came."

"Nobody came?"

"No one thought to come and see me," June said, her voice rising slightly. "No one from that church, where I'd paid my pledge for so long. So I never went back there. I couldn't."

"I'm so sorry. Did you ever tell the church why you left?"

"Tell them? Why should I tell them? They should have known."

"It seems like they didn't know."

"What's your point?"

"Maybe if the people at the church had known you were hurting, they would have done something to correct it."

"I didn't need them."

"But I thought—I see. Okay."

"I shouldn't talk about this," June said. "I'm sorry. You should go."

"I'm sorry if I—"

"You should go."

I considered the untouched glasses of iced tea sweating on the cocktail table between us. I wanted to take June's hands in mine and say a prayer so right that as soon as I'd uttered "Amen," the doorbell would ring and God would be standing there, trim and timely as a UPS deliveryman, and I would make my graceful exit, leaving June to delight in the contents of the package she had just signed for. Instead, I said, "I'll go," and left.

I saw June a few times after that, at her home, because she rarely attended worship. On my second visit we both acted embarrassed and apologetic about the way our relationship had begun. Then we acted forgiving and fond, and a bond formed between us. I became the young lady who did right by June, who kept showing up for her, who didn't forget.

Until I forgot. I once neglected to visit June in the hospital at the hour we'd agreed on, and then when I did finally show up, bearing a ridiculous consolation gift—a small vase of artificial pink roses complete with counterfeit dewdrops glued to the petals—June's soft, pained face clearly told me, *I thought you were different, but you're not. You're no different. Leave me alone.*

Back when I was a pastor-in-training I thought preaching would be the hardest part of ministry. How, how on earth would I climb into a pulpit week after week and attempt to proclaim God's Word in a manner that had any meaning for the people in the pews? Not only would I have to have prepared a decent sermon, but by Sunday morning at ten I'd have to surmount my internal terrors and conquer my ghastly attack of Lord's Day diarrhea. Then I learned that pastoral visitation can be a more formidable task than preaching. Whereas the preacher is protected by the pulpit, the sermon manuscript, and the congregational custom of respectful listening, for the pastoral care provider no such protections exist. It's just you and June and her loneliness, her anger, her colossal, insoluble grief.

After being discharged from the hospital, June retreated into self-imposed exile, declining my offers of pastoral visits and staying away from church altogether. The desert city where June and I both live is home to increasing numbers of senior citizens, many of whom, like June, have outlived their spouses, and in some cases even their children.

Over the years of my ministry in Tucson, I've encountered numerous women and men who, not unlike the desert elders Abba Antony once described, spend their days practicing a solitude less serene than it appears: "He who sits alone and is quiet," said Antony, "has escaped from three wars: hearing, speaking, seeing: but there is one thing against which he must continually fight: that is, his own heart." If I could have, I would have somehow introduced June to a few of her

peers—other solitary seniors I'd met along the way, also rav-
aged by loss and disappointed by the faulty Christians on
whom they'd hoped to depend in their late years. People like
June should depend on each other, I thought. They should form
co-ops and communes instead of staying home alone, dutifully
mailing their monthly pledge checks to churches they refuse
to attend. It frightened and saddened me to think of June in
her mustard-colored chair, doing silent battle with her heart,
without so much as a lapdog for company.

But the truth is, June chose to be alone. She chose her
interior desert, and if she had anything to say about it, she
would die in her own damned house. She would have no truck
with some groovy utopia where all the lonely people found
friendship. Besides, no such place exists. Even the Activities
Director of a posh condo complex for retirees tells me that
the residents crave deeper relationships than their daily pleas-
antries in the sunlit atrium allow. They moved into the place
to claim its promised "Independent Senior Living," but now
they're getting what they paid for, and it's not really what they
want. What they want may look less like independence than
dignified dependence—dependence on someone dependable,
someone who'll know enough to show up when you're hurting, someone who'll stick around, who won't just go and die
on you like that.

– Day 39 –
The Enemy in Question

Abba Zeno said, "If a man wants God to hear his prayer quickly, then before he prays for anything else, even his own soul, when he stands and stretches out his hands towards God, he must pray with all his heart for his enemies. Through this action God will hear everything that he asks."

The Sayings of the Desert Fathers, 67

In September of 2006, Pope Benedict XVI publicly quoted a fourteenth-century Christian emperor who said, "Show me just what Mohammed brought that was new and there you will find things only evil and inhuman, such as his command to spread by the sword the faith he preached."[29] The Pope spoke these words amid an academic speech intended to point out that reason, and not violence, pleases God. A firestorm of controversy—and violence—erupted in the Muslim world. Many offended people felt the Pope was insensitive to the realities and concerns of modern Muslims. Others believed the Pope's remarks had been taken out of context and misunderstood.

A Muslim friend of mine e-mailed me, saying of the Pope, "I feel for the guy. It's not easy being infallible. I mean, can't a person make a mistake without a reaction at this level? I'm concerned about all these Muslims who are resorting to violence.

They're fulfilling the stereotype of Muslims as violent." She added, "Many non-Muslims don't understand how deeply Muslims revere their Prophet Mohammed."

Not long thereafter, a member of the church I serve approached me with an offer, a request: she wished to make a presentation for adults of the church on militancy within Islam. She is soft-spoken, gracious, and articulate, with snowy hair and fashionable eyeglass frames. Since September 11, 2001, she has read extensively on the subject of Islamic extremism. She proposed to facilitate a discussion entitled "After 9/11: Fears, Facts, and Going Forward."

I wanted to welcome the woman and her wisdom, but I also knew that, lest we inadvertently create an atmosphere conducive to ethnic stereotyping and religious intolerance, any discussion of Muslim fundamentalism and terrorism must occur only after the people of the church had been made familiar with what I came to term "the basics and beautiful aspects of Islam."

I invited a guest speaker, an Egyptian-born, hijab-wearing graduate student in her mid-thirties, to introduce the roughly thirty Christians in attendance to the five pillars of Islam and related themes. With great generosity of spirit our guest talked about her religion and her community. After she had finished describing the Muslim profession of faith, prayer practices, fasting, almsgiving, and pilgrimage to Mecca, one of the Presbyterians present said, "This faith you're describing is nothing like what we hear about in the media." Following our guest's presentation, the person who lingered the longest, chatting with her, was the Jewish husband of a church member.

The following week, the "After 9/11" discussion took place, and was just as well attended as the previous week's event had been. The leader began by asking us to name, in very brief phrases, what our immediate responses to 9/11 had been. I served as a scribe, writing in large letters on newsprint posters such words as "shock," "horror," and "punish them." I appreciated the honesty of the participants and the leader's ability to move the conversation from gut reactions to the carefully researched information she presented on the history and development of Muslim militancy.

Eventually, some of those present talked about practical Christian responses to the problem, such as establishing missions supportive of infrastructure-building and educational development in impoverished, largely Muslim nations, where despair often gives rise to religious fanaticism. While an unspoken premise of the conversation was surely that terrorists are "our enemies," only one person in attendance seemed at all anxious to arrive at "us-versus-them" conclusions.

"If a man wants God to hear his prayer quickly, then before he prays for anything else, even his own soul, when he stands and stretches out his hands towards God, he must pray with all his heart for his enemies." Thus says Abba Zeno, a contemplative, nomadic Christian of the fifth century who practiced his faith in Egypt, Syria, and Palestine, eventually settling near Gaza. Wise though he was, it is doubtful that Zeno could have conceived that a third, monotheistic religion, following Judaism and Christianity, would flourish in his homelands centuries after his lifetime. Even more unthinkable to Zeno than the rise of Islam would be its deadly bastardization by a minority of hell-bent fundamentalists of the twentieth and twenty-first centuries.

What Zeno did understand, at a level deeper and more enduring than the particular vicissitudes of history, was the reality of enemies. Enemies happen. Enmity inevitably happens between human beings, and even touches those rare souls who take up residence in the severe and prayer-inducing landscapes of the earth in order to devote their lives to God. Thus Abba Zeno's ancient insight applies to the present moment, and to any moment. We must pray for our enemies. Doing so deepens our own relationships with God.

Generally, those present at my church for the "After 9/11" presentation projected the sincere and baffled demeanor I have seen many times among Christians trying to fathom the motivations of a suicide bomber. Of course, comprehending one's enemies is essential to effectively combating them. But for Abba Zeno and for those who would learn from him, the enemy in question dwells within the Christian soul.

If, as a Christian, I want to draw closer to God, I must overcome my temptation to segregate my prayers, to exclude my enemies from them. When I forget or refuse to pray for my enemies, I fashion at best a partial image of God; I imagine a selective deity whose interests are restricted to my own. Zeno implies that God is slow to hear prayers so narrowly conceived. God is quick to hear the prayers of the faithful who are willing to seek blessings for their most fearsome, least deserving adversaries. God is eager to respond to people who are sufficiently humble to let God be who God is: the unconditional lover and immeasurably merciful redeemer of all creation, all humankind.

− Day 40 −
Afterwards

Amma Syncletica said, "In the beginning there are a great many
battles and a good deal of suffering for those who are advancing
towards God and afterwards, ineffable joy. It is like those who wish
to light a fire; at first they are choked by the smoke and cry . . . .
So we also must kindle the divine fire in ourselves through tears
and hard work."

The Forgotten Desert Mothers, 43

Last night, in the elegant, modern sanctuary of an Epis-
copal church, I stood before roughly twenty-five adults, having
been invited to teach a class on "The Wisdom of the Desert
Christians." I told the students about how the Emperor Constantine's fourth-century baptism had radically altered Christianity, exposing it to the light of the Roman day, eventually
driving many Christians to flee from the empire's corrupting
excesses and seek the obscurity and deprivations of the desert.
I explained that, much as these Desert Christians represented
an important historical and religious movement, they were
not monolithic, but diverse: women and men, rich, poor, and
middle-income, learned and illiterate, tradesfolk and heirs.

"They sought," I said, "what you and I seek: to be transformed by God through prayer. They practiced asceticism:

intentional simplicity, nonattachment to the self-aggrandizing values of the dominant culture. They were minimalists who fasted for the purpose of clearing away obstructions on the path to God.

"The Desert Christians cultivated acute self-awareness and inner equilibrium. They sought to live in emotional balance, in harmony with creation and other human beings. They practiced solitude and silence, but they also offered hospitality and kindness to the pilgrims who sought their counsel.

"They were grounded in Scripture and they prayed," I said, "long and hard. They thirsted for God. On their way to transformation and salvation, they were willing to endure great spiritual dryness. They persevered, and because they did, we're still learning from them today."

The class participants paid gracious attention to my words. Some talked about how the Arizona desert had given them a taste for solitude and silence. One man spoke in ominous tones, suggesting that if we failed to learn from our Desert Christian forebears we would be no better off than the citizens of Rome. The woman seated beside him told this story:

> The first time I saw the desert, I was just a little girl. My dad had sold the farm in Ireland—which I could still kill him for doing, by the way—to take a big American vacation. So there we were, on a train to California, and the desert outside the train windows astounded me. My dad kept saying, "goddamn *wasteland*," but I was enthralled. And now, the desert teaches me subtlety. There are so many different shades of green in the vegetation here, if you'll just look for them. It makes me think of what subtle things the Spirit might also be doing inside me.

At the end of the evening an unsmiling woman with leathery skin softly croaked, "The Spirit breathes in us, and we're changed."

True enough, but some things never change. To paraphrase a bit of Buddhist wisdom—*After the ecstasy, the laundry*—after the closing prayer, the folding chairs. We cleaned up the place, bid one another good night, and, each in our separate vehicles, drove out into the desert darkness that amateur astronomers cherish and county legislators protect with light-pollution laws.

Heading eastward through the blackness, I thought about the names of the intersecting roads where the church was located: La Cholla and Tangerine. These typified the desert where I live, with its prickly, indigenous species as well as its juicy transplants.

How had I come to be transplanted from Chicago, that grinding, Midwestern metropolis subject to "lake effects," to Tucson, this city surrounded by mountains that go pink at dusk, where cacti flourish in a thousand subtle shades of green? And how had I come to teach other Christians anything—I, who, as a rather confused young adult some twenty years earlier, had done the Constantinian thing, and been baptized?

"In the beginning," Amma Syncletica said, "there are a great many battles and a good deal of suffering for those who are advancing towards God." I see Syncletica's point. For roughly eight years after the baptismal waters had dried on my skin, externally, I went about my life as if all was more or less well. But internally I wandered in a desert into which I felt I had been enticed, as Gomer, the prophet Hosea's "wife of whoredom," was lured into the wilderness by God's tender words (Hosea 2:14). I felt I had entered a long, parched, and pointless Lent. During this period of doubt and discernment all I truly needed was given to me, but who wants what they need? We want what we want. *Goddamn wasteland*, I thought. I was itchy and restless as a snake that has outgrown its skin. I wanted to shake, once and for all, my memory of God's alluring voice and the baffling baptism I had undergone.

"We need nothing of what we left behind," Amma Syncletica once said. "There we had reputation and plenty to eat; here we have little to eat and not much of anything else."[30]

I yearned to retrieve my former life and its comforts. Amid my deep second thoughts about having been buried, baptismally, with Christ, I wrote:

From you, who lured me into this exile,
I take back my prayers.
I give back your answers; they're killing me.
Please. I could eat my own words,
I'm so hungry.

God, true to form, neither gave back my prayers nor took back the answers. And so I live a desert life now. I'm a hybrid creature, I suppose: part tangerine and part cholla cactus, part ripened and tender, part thorny and defended. This is to say that like you, and like that cussing Irish farmer on a westbound American train, and even a little like Syncletica, I'm human— contradictory, yet surely beloved of God. And like you, I'm making my way through a world that often looks like a godforsaken wasteland. You and I may sometimes seem to be driving through darkness that's endless. But I believe Syncletica when she says there is an end to all of this. Surely we're advancing toward God. And afterwards, ineffable joy.

Notes

[1] *Saint Benedict's Rule: A New Translation for Today*, trans. Patrick Barry, OSB (York: Ampleforth Abbey Press, 1997), 89.

[2] *The Sayings of the Desert Fathers: The Alphabetical Collection*, trans. Benedicta Ward, SLG (Kalamazoo, MI: Cistercian Publications, 1975), 231.

[3] Frank M. Snowden Jr., *Before Color Prejudice: The Ancient View of Blacks* (Cambridge, MA: Harvard University Press, 1983), quoted in http://resolutereader.blogspot.com/2007/06/frank-m-snowden-jr-before-color.html.

[4] Amma Syncletica, http://dailydesertwisdom.blogspot.com/2007/08/patience-of-moses.html.

[5] Brian Noell, "Race in Late Antique Egypt: Moses the Black and Authentic Historical Voice," *Eras* (Edition 6, November 2004), http://arts.monash.edu.au/eras/edition_6/noellarticle.htm.

[6] "Paris Hilton: *People's* Exclusive Interview," *People*, June 27, 2007. http://www.people.com/people/article/0,,20041406_20043875,00.html.

[7] "Paris Hilton on 'Larry King Live,'" CNN.com (June 28, 2007), http://www.cnn.com/2007/SHOWBIZ/TV/06/27/king.hilton.transcript/index.html.

[8] "Navajo Cleansing Ceremony Held in Dorm Where Teen Slain," *News from Indian Country* (September 2007), http://indiancountrynews.net/index.php?option=com_content&task=view&id=1381&Itemid=1.

[9] *Guest Book for Mia Henderson*, Legacy.com (2007), http://www.legacy.com/AZCentral/GB/GuestbookView.aspx?PersonId=93931636.

[10] Ibid.

150   *City of Prayer*

[11] Ibid.

[12] Ibid.

[13] Felicia Fonseca, "Recent Killing Prompts Navajo Worry over Loss of Culture," *ABQJournal.com* (September 7, 2007), http://www.abqjournal.com/news/state/aptribal09-07-07.htm?splashtop.

[14] *The Book of Mystical Chapters: Meditations on the Soul's Ascent from the Desert Fathers and Other Early Christian Contemplatives*, trans. John Anthony McGuckin (Boston: Shambhala Publications, 2003), 60.

[15] "Suspect in UA Killing Had No History of Violence, Mother Says," *KTAR.com* (September 6, 2007), http://news.ktar.com/?nid=6&sid=586327.

[16] Al Durtschi, "An Introduction to the Navajo Culture," http://waltonfeed.com/peoples/navajo/culture.html.

[17] Ibid.

[18] The Chauvins, "Be Still," *Guest Book for Mia Henderson* (September 14, 2007), http://www.legacy.com/AZCentral/GB/GuestbookView.aspx?PersonId=93931636&PageNo=3.

[19] Derwas James Chitty, *The Desert a City: An Introduction to the Study of Egyptian and Palestinian Monasticism Under the Christian Empire* (Crestwood, NY: St. Vladimir's Seminary Press, 1966), 71–72.

[20] Joel Felix, in "Ralph J. Mills, Jr.," by Tom Raworth (August, 2007), http://www.tomraworth.com/rjm.html.

[21] Ralph J. Mills, Jr., "You," in *Grasses Standing: Selected Poems* (Kingston, RI: Moyer Bell, 2000), 17.

[22] Helen Mills, unpublished letter to Peter Manson, quoted by Tom Raworth, http://www.tomraworth.com/rjm.html.

[23] G.0106b., *Book of Order*, Presbyterian Church USA.

[24] Peter J. Gomes, http://www.philosophy-religion.org/handouts/homophobic.htm.

[25] Peter J. Gomes, "Homophobia," *The Public Forum* (The American Psychoanalytic Foundation, 1999), http://cyberpsych.org/homophobia/noframes/gomes.htm.

[26] Warren Johansson and William A. Percy, "Homosexuality in the Middle Ages," http://www.williamapercy.com/wiki/index.php/Homosexuality_in_the_Middle_Ages.

[27] Ibid.

[28] "The Gift of Love," words by Hal Hopson (Carol Stream, IL: Hope Publishing, 1972). All rights reserved. Used by permission.

[29] Benedict XVI, "Faith, Reason and the University: Memories and Reflections," *Lecture of the Holy Father* (September 12, 2006), http://www.vatican.va/holy_father/benedict_xvi/speeches/2006/september/documents/hf_ben-xvi_spe_20060912_university-regensburg_en.html.

[30] Benedicta Ward, ed., *The Desert Fathers: Sayings of the Early Christian Monks* (London: Penguin, 2003), 143.

Bibliography

Swan, Laura. *The Forgotten Desert Mothers: Sayings, Lives and Stories of Early Christian Women.* Mahwah, NJ: Paulist Press, 2001.

Ward, Benedicta, ed. *The Sayings of the Desert Fathers: The Alphabetical Collection.* Kalamazoo, MI: Cistercian Publications, 1975.

———. *The Desert Fathers: Sayings of the Early Christian Monks.* London: Penguin Books, 2003.